Michael Mangis

SIGNATURE SINS

Taming Our Wayward Hearts

IVP Books

An imprint of InterVarsity Press
Downers Grove, Illinois

InterVarsity Press
P.O. Box 1400, Downers Grove, IL 60515-1426
World Wide Web: www.ivpress.com
Email: email@ivpress.com

InterVarsity Press® *is the book-publishing division of InterVarsity Christian Fellowship/USA*®, *a student movement active on campus at hundreds of universities, colleges and schools of nursing in the United States of America, and a member movement of the International Fellowship of Evangelical Students. For information about local and regional activities, write Public Relations Dept., InterVarsity Christian Fellowship/USA, 6400 Schroeder Rd., P.O. Box 7895, Madison, WI 53707-7895, or visit the IVCF website at <www.intervarsity.org>.*

All Scripture quotations, unless otherwise indicated, are taken from the Holy Bible, New International Version®. NIV®. *Copyright* ©*1973, 1978, 1984 by International Bible Society. Used by permission of Zondervan Publishing House. All rights reserved.*

The song "Generations" by Sara Groves, quoted on p. 121, is ©*1999 Sara Groves Music (admin. by Music Services). All rights reserved. ASCAP.*

Design: Cindy Kiple
Images: iStockphoto

ISBN 978-0-8308-3515-7

Printed in the United States of America ∞

Library of Congress Cataloging-in-Publication Data

Mangis, Michael W., 1962-
  Signature sins: taming our wayward hearts / Michael W. Mangis.
    p. cm.
  Includes bibliographical references and index.
  ISBN 978-0-8308-3515-7 (pbk.: alk. paper)
  1. Sin—Christianity. 2. Christian life. I. Title.
  BT715.M2795 2008
  241'.3—dc22

                    2008022651

P 21 20 19 18 17 16 15 14 13 12 11 10 9 8 7 6 5 4 3 2 1
Y 25 24 23 22 21 20 19 18 17 16 15 14 13 12 11 10 09 08

"After embracing Christ's death as paying the penalty for our sins, Christians embark on a life of discipleship and growth by which we can experience increasing freedom from the bondage and power of sin. *Signature Sins* offers us insights from Scripture, tradition and contemporary psychology that illuminate that path of growth, helping us to see the patterns of our failings and offering us possibilities for increasing freedom."

STANTON L. JONES, PROVOST, WHEATON COLLEGE, AND AUTHOR OF *EX-GAYS?*

"Michael Mangis is a subtle prophet-sage, confronting our sin while gently steering us between the shoals of legalistic sin management and psychological excuse making. His book is marked by beautiful contrasts: deep but simple, ancient but fresh; it is good integration that takes the Bible seriously. The author accomplishes a lot in a small space, combining practical spiritual direction with the insights of a Christian dynamic therapy. This will be useful for laypersons and pastors, counselors and their counselees, directors and their friends."

ERIC JOHNSON, DIRECTOR, SOCIETY FOR CHRISTIAN PSYCHOLOGY, AND AUTHOR OF *FOUNDATIONS FOR SOUL CARE*

"Michael Mangis says he wants to induce excitement on our Christian journey, not guilt or gloom. That is difficult to do in a book about sin, but he succeeds by helping us to recognize that sin is far more complex and grace is far more dynamic than we might have thought. By constantly reminding us that one size doesn't fit all, Mangis draws on Scripture and the Christian tradition, anecdotes from his own life and his practice as a psychotherapist, and a reservoir of helpful analogies to engage readers in an eminently practical and thoughtful examination of their own spiritual health with prescriptive suggestions for hearts that are prone to wander. What I found encouraging was his ability to integrate insights from the field of psychology with an honesty and humility that refrains from making Christianity obsequious to the social sciences."

DENNIS OKHOLM, PROFESSOR OF THEOLOGY, AZUSA PACIFIC UNIVERSITY, AND AUTHOR OF *MONK HABITS FOR EVERYDAY PEOPLE*

"Drawing wisdom from the worlds of both psychotherapy and spiritual direction, this introductory overview of vital disciplines for the Christian's inner life is clear, strong and robustly down-to-earth. Especially salutary is Mangis's stress on finding and fighting one's own core sin."

J. I. PACKER, PROFESSOR OF THEOLOGY, REGENT COLLEGE, AND AUTHOR OF *KNOWING GOD*

"Michael Mangis has provided an excellent resource for soul-care professionals and laity. *Signature Sins* is honest, comprehensive and accessible. Few writers could offer the blending of psychological scholarship and theological sophistication in a style that is warm and approachable."

GARY W. MOON, EXECUTIVE EDITOR, *CONVERSATIONS*, AND AUTHOR OF *FALLING FOR GOD*

"I often hear people distinguish between wisdom and knowledge. Michael W. Mangis brings the two together—in his personal life, in his teaching and now in this remarkable book, *Signature Sins*. Read this book. It is deeply informative, spiritually inspiring, written with clarity, filled with practical questions for self-reflection and saturated with an awareness of God's grace."

MARK R. MCMINN, PROFESSOR OF PSYCHOLOGY, GEORGE FOX UNIVERSITY, AND AUTHOR OF *SIN AND GRACE IN CHRISTIAN COUNSELING*

This book is dedicated to my wife, Patricia Hughes Mangis.

The heart of this book has grown from our conversations and from leading spiritual formation groups together.

More importantly, Patti, your love, commitment and faithfulness have given me the courage to know myself more honestly and to seek to know God more honestly too. Your persistent, unflinching quest for righteousness is an inspiration to me and to others. You are always patient to wait for God's will to be resolved. Since my stroke, your faith in God's perfect providence and plan for my future has held me together.

This book would not exist without you, and for these and other reasons, it is dedicated to you.

Contents

I

Why Do We Sin?

WHEN I WAS GROWING UP IN A conservative Protestant church, I did not question the assumption that I sinned. Far too many sermons assured me of that reality. I was comforted to know that all the other members of the congregation belonged to the same club of sinners. The only difference was the degree to which our sins showed. Some people were better than others at keeping their sins under control.

Through sermons and Sunday school lessons I learned that the Bible was filled with all manner of troubles for those who did not manage their sins well enough. Sin was some kind of wild beast that I had to keep on a very short leash. I could keep it under control, but I would never entirely banish that dangerous part of myself. I shuddered to think what would happen if the beast got loose.

WE SIN BECAUSE WE ARE SINFUL?

Just as it never occurred to me to doubt that I was a sinner, I never wondered aloud *why* I sinned. The reason for our sin was another common sermon subject. We sin because we are born with original sin. We have inherited the curse of the Fall in the Garden of Eden. Satan's sin was pride; he wanted to put himself in the place of God. When we sin, we are doing exactly what Satan did. In our pride we want to play God and run our lives in our own way.

The reasoning was circular. In essence I was being taught that we sin because we are sinful. If we sin out of the pride of wanting to be like God, that only brings us back to an infinite chicken-and-egg loop. Pride *is* a sin. So we sin because we are sinful. It wasn't enough to satisfy me.

In addition to the circular reasoning, original sin struck me as extremely unfair. Should we inherit Adam's curse and be condemned for choices he and Eve made? If I asked about it at church, I was told that it didn't matter, because if we had been there we would have done exactly the same thing.

Today the preteens in my Sunday school class ask the same questions I asked as a child, and I struggle to answer them. I have never stopped asking the questions for myself. As a clinical psychologist I have spent a great deal of time over the years asking *Why do we sin?*

The debate over free will and original sin is centuries old. Augustine, following Paul, taught that all humankind is born in a state of original sin, and all require God's grace to be saved. The fourth-century monk Pelagius made a different argument, that only Adam was affected by Adam's sin. Pelagius taught that every newborn child is born a clean slate and does not suffer the effects of sin until taught to sin. Pelagius was proclaimed a heretic. Since that time the Western church has rejected pelagianism in its purest form. No belief system can legitimately be called Christian unless it acknowledges that every human is sinful and in need of salvation.

Even if we accept that we are born tainted by original sin, there is room left over for free will and responsibility in the specific ways that we choose to sin. More central to the discussion of this book, there is room left over for the reasons why we choose our particular sins.

NO RANDOM SINS
My life, like my home, carries unique markers of my own experiences,

relationships, likes, dislikes, gifts and vices. My life displays patterns, consistencies and habits. Even spontaneity occurs within boundaries.

My sin is similarly patterned. I can predict my temptations by the choices that have enticed me before. Other temptations may afflict my neighbor but cause me no struggle at all. My patterns of sin are unique to me.

Most of us are not tossed about by temptations like winds from every direction. Few people are tempted one day by drunkenness and the next day by sexual immorality and the next day by stealing or violence or sloth. We do not sin at random. Our sin takes a consistent and predictable course.

In his wonderful book *The Return of the Prodigal Son*, Henri Nouwen expresses our universal experience of empathy with the lost son in Jesus' parable (Lk 15:11-32). In his pride and greed the younger son asks to receive his inheritance early, essentially expressing the wish that his father was dead. After squandering the father's gift, the son reaches a point of such desperation that he starts for home, where he hopes to again benefit from his father's generosity and live as a servant. The father, who has been continually scanning the horizon for his son, runs out to greet him with open arms and reinstates him as a son. The older brother resents the father's lavish display of grace. He expresses his frustration that the father showered such favor on the disobedient son when he, the faithful son, deserved it so much more. The father reminds his eldest that he had always enjoyed the gift of sonship. What more is there to celebrate? The younger brother had lost his place at the father's side and has now regained it. His restoration is worthy of the most extravagant party!

For Nouwen and for most of us, it is not so much the decadence and sinful abandon of the prodigal that we identify with; instead we recognize ourselves in his desire to be welcomed by the father with open arms—to come home. Who does not long for that kind of welcoming embrace?

Our empathy with the prodigal son expresses the universal human feeling of homelessness. We have all felt as we imagine the prodigal felt, alone and overwhelmed. Wouldn't it be wonderful to find our way home and see a loved one come running out on the road to meet us, to receive us and celebrate us?

God's love is that kind of love. We are that beloved. No matter the extent of our sin, our Father welcomes us with enthusiasm.

As Nouwen explored his own life, he came to admit what is probably true for most of us. He found that although he empathized with the prodigal son, it was the older brother that he most resembled. The brother is annoyed at the grace lavished on the returning prodigal. The older brother has been outwardly obedient to all the father asked. Because of his obedience, he expects to be treated better than the prodigal. His reaction reveals the pride and self-righteousness deeply rooted in his heart. He focuses on the outward visible sin of his lost brother and fails to see the inward sin of his own pride.

I repeat the sin of the older brother when I keep my eyes on others' sin in order to feel better about my own spiritual report card. My struggle with inward, silent sins is less troubling when I remember the drunkenness and sexual immorality of the neighbor down the street.

It is no small irony that although I resemble the older brother of Jesus' parable much more closely than I resemble the prodigal son, like Nouwen I feel most like the prodigal. I want the best of both worlds, to feel superior like the elder and to feel welcomed home like the younger.

Like the older brother, I am often jealous of those who tell of dramatic conversions from lives of sin. Many of us who have grown up being outwardly good have testimony envy toward those whose conversion stories are more dramatic. It is easy to forget what the father said to his eldest son. "'My son,' the father said, 'you are always with me, and everything I have is yours. But we had to celebrate and be glad, because this brother of yours was dead and is alive again; he was lost and is found'" (Lk 15:31-32).

The two brothers sinned in different ways. One, lost to his own sensual passions, sought after every pleasure the world had to offer. The other managed his outward behavior well but harbored inner sins reflective of his own character.

Many of Jesus' parables and teachings reveal his understanding that fallen human nature wants to place greater emphasis on the outward life than on the heart. Jesus called his listeners to the more difficult inner search of the soul.

A Sin Signature

Our sins are not unique. The writer of Ecclesiastes said, "There is nothing new under the sun" (Eccles 1:9). The apostle Paul wrote, "No temptation has seized you except what is common to man" (1 Cor 10:13). Tradition has even organized human sins into seven deadly categories. In all our individuality we still sin in the same ways people have sinned since the fall of Adam and Eve.

Although my sins are not new, they assert their presence in my life in unique ways. I personally struggle with pride. Pride is universal and is a central sin, but my own personal pride takes on patterns and subtleties that make it uniquely mine.

My gender influences the ways I exhibit pride. So do my culture and my religious upbringing. My relational history has formed the personality hungers and needs that I attempt to satisfy through my pride, and my family teaches me how to try to satisfy those needs and hungers. Even my biological temperament influences the ways my pride takes shape.

The writer of Hebrews speaks of persistent personal sins and how we must combat them. "Let us throw off everything that hinders and the sin that so easily entangles" (Heb 12:1). The Revised Standard Version phrases it "sin which clings so closely." Historically our persistent sins were called *besetting sins* from the King James Version: "the sin which doth so easily beset us." No matter how it is worded, the phrase suggests a type of sin with a quality of such nearness that we forget it is there. I picture something like spandex. I don't notice it until I take a step and it pulls me in the wrong direction and causes me to stumble. Jesus used the analogy of yeast in bread dough. Sin suffuses itself throughout our beings and cannot be separated from the other ingredients.

SPIRITUAL SIBLINGS

Paul taught that our clinging sins are an inescapable curse of the Fall and its resulting law of sin. "I find this law at work: When I want to do good, evil is right there with me" (Rom 7:21). Sin is like a tight membrane that becomes nearly indistinguishable from my skin. Out of universal categories I craft a web of sin that is mine in particular. There is no temptation except what is common to all humanity, yet individuality asserts itself in the ways I respond to every temptation.

Like a signature, my sin pattern is so characteristic of me that it could be used to identify me. It's my sin profile. Anyone who knows me intimately would instantly recognize it as mine. That is why I strive to keep it hidden, even overcompensate for it, so that not even my most intimate companions would suspect that it is there. I invest great energy into presenting a façade—a false front or mask—calculated to eliminate all evidence of my profile of sin.

The seduction of false belief comes in the form of two central human struggles: pride and fear. The fear of mortality drives us to deny Christ's humanity—the heresy of Docetism. We want Christ to be untouched by the corruption of humanness, just as we want to escape it ourselves. At the other extreme, pride in our humanness leads us to deny Christ's divinity—the heresy of Adoptionism. With Lucifer, we resent the fact that Christ has been elevated above us, and we crave equality with him.

Pride and fear are interesting spiritual siblings. There is something elemental about them and the way we humans vacillate between them. Each drives us to sin in different ways. At one moment my pride pushes me to grasp beyond what God has put within my reach. At the very next moment I fear God's rejection and abandonment and want him to rescue me. Pride and fear lie at the heart of original sin.

CORRALLING THE MARBLES

In his examination of Jesus' Sermon on the Mount, Dallas Willard notes that the church often fails to point believers toward a richer life of the soul and instead preaches "gospels of sin management." Rather than rooting out our sins, we try to keep them under control. Managing sin is like playing with one of those puzzles with tiny metal marbles in a maze. I am trying to get all the marbles corralled into one little area. Just when I have almost accomplished the task, a marble pops out of place. When at last I have all the marbles in place—all my sins under control—Jesus tells me that there are marbles that I had forgotten even existed.

The appeal of the gospel of sin management is that once I have my outer life under some degree of control, I can feel free to turn my attention to the mess that others have made of their lives. Never mind that my inner life may be a quagmire of filth or, worse, an empty wasteland. At least I look good on the outside. Jesus accused the Pharisees of the same attitude when he said, "You are like whitewashed tombs, which look beautiful on the outside but on the inside are full of dead men's bones and everything unclean" (Mt 23:27).

When we abandon the idea of sin as failure to manage external behavior and look at sin as a failure of our soul to be fully attuned to God's soul, we can let go of the compulsive practice of speck spotting. Jesus asked, "Why do you look at the speck of sawdust in your brother's eye and pay no attention to the plank in your own eye?" (Mt 7:3). Not only must I give up the guilty pleasure of comparing the quality of my sin management to that of others, but I must begin to face up to my responsibility for my own sin.

In Jesus' scheme of things, the purpose of getting my own life in order is not to give me an opportunity to feel self-important but to call me to care for the poor, the lonely, the bereaved and all others who do not have the luxury of keeping their lives whitewashed on the outside. Jesus taught that the sinner's humble prayer for mercy is more welcome to God's ears than the bragging of those who think they have managed their sins (Lk 18:9-14).

A rich young man came to Jesus and asked, "What must I do to inherit eternal life?" The young man reported that he had kept all of God's commandments since he was a child. "Jesus looked at him and loved him. 'One thing you lack,' he said. 'Go, sell everything you have and give to the poor, and you will have treasure in heaven. Then come, follow me.' At this the man's face fell. He went away sad, because he had great wealth" (Mk 10:21-22). Like that young man, in pride I may come to Jesus to have my righteousness praised, only to have the Lord zoom in on a key area where my heart is unwilling to submit.

For nearly two decades I have worshiped in an Episcopal congregation. When I first participated in the liturgy, the prayer of confession in preparation for the Eucharist powerfully struck me. "Most merciful God, we confess that we have sinned against you in thought, word, and deed, by what we have done, *and by what we have left undone.* We have not loved you with our whole heart; we have not loved our neighbors as ourselves."

No matter how hard I work to manage my behavioral sins of *commission*, it is impossible for me to keep all the commandments. The sins of *omission* remain. I do not love God with my whole heart; I do not love my neighbor as myself. There is always at least one marble rattling around loose.

THE PERSISTENT THORN

Every sin confessed is an invitation for God to work miracles through his grace. If I truly grasped this truth, I would stop obsessively working to round up all my sin marbles and keep them under control. Instead I would go out in search of marbles that are lost or forgotten in the corners of my heart. I might actually become bored with the areas of my life that are tidy and presentable. I would search out new places in me that haven't seen the full light of God's transformation. I might even think, *It has been a while since God performed a miracle in me. Let me find a forgotten pocket of sin somewhere so I can set God's power free to turn water into wine and blindness into sight.*

When we consider our signature sins, we should also consider the biological roots of who we are and how we interact with the world. In addition to obvious struggles like mental illness or brain damage, we should take into account our biological temperament. Some people have a natural tendency toward anxiety, anger or depression. These tendencies often run in families. Some people will never struggle with the sin of anger; in fact I have patients for whom a good dose of healthy anger is a goal of their therapy. I have others who are addicted to anger; if they allow it into their hearts at all it will take residence for days before they can get it under control. Their temperament, partly biological, gives them a constant boost in an angry direction. They are no weaker or more sinful than the next person; they simply have a different cross to bear.

The apostle Paul confessed to such a personal struggle when he wrote of his thorn in the flesh (2 Cor 12:7-10). Many have wondered exactly what thorn Paul struggled with. A friend of mine suggested that it may have been guilt and shame over the many believers Paul had killed in his pre-conversion life. Whatever his struggle, Paul emphasized both God's grace being the only thing sufficient to confront our weakness and God's purpose in using our weaknesses to humble us and glorify himself. When we administer grace to one in pain, we embody Christ for that person. When we allow struggles to turn us toward God we redeem the brokenness.

HONESTY OVER IMAGE

When we reject the false legalism of sin management under the law and turn to the freedom of the miraculous power of God's grace, we are attending to *spiritual formation*. In recent years the ancient writings and practices of spiritual direction have enjoyed a renaissance. Courses and study programs in spiritual formation have sprung up everywhere, and for good reason. The contemporary believer and seeker alike have grown weary of the superficiality of our culture and of the common church. We know there must be more than pretending to be good enough.

The secular priesthood of psychotherapy cannot offer meaning beyond the level of behavior. Self-awareness for its own sake brings little satisfaction. To know my heart is a start, but it leads nowhere if I cannot then open those newly discovered rooms to the light of God's transformation.

The religious priesthood and pastorate have done little better than the secular. Most congregations do not create a welcoming space for the confession of sin. Those in power often present themselves as icons of near-perfection. The common sinner, who cannot manage to hide sins so well, is left feeling inferior. When we do confess our sins in church, they are usually the small and acceptable sins. The implication—that these are the only marbles left outside of the corral—makes us look better than if we pretended to have no sins at all.

The hunger for deeper spiritual formation cannot be satisfied in communities that value image over honesty. We must reject the gospel of sin management and embrace the gospel of grace. We are on a pilgrimage in the truest sense of that word. The pilgrim seeks to be transformed by the journey into one worthy of arriving at the destination. The pain of encountering ourselves and naming our signature sins fades in comparison with the joy of the transformation that occurs. Pilgrims long to know their signature sins so they may willingly submit them to Christ's healing touch.

AN "INCURABLE SUSPICION"

Oswald Chambers brilliantly pointed out that the root of sin lies in "an incurable suspicion of God": the suspicion that God is not good. My signature sins are my personal doubts about God's goodness. I sin when I do not trust that God has my best interests at heart. I sin when I am alone and afraid and God's promises seem so long ago and difficult to remember. I sin when I am pretty sure that God would say no to the thing I want right now but that I am convinced I cannot live without.

My wife was on a vacation in England. She was staying at an inn, and every day she walked into town by the same route. On the return walk she always came to a confusing intersection. On the first day she took the wrong turn and had to retrace her steps to get back on the right path. For several days afterward she took the same wrong turn because it looked so familiar. The wrong way looked more convincing than the right way.

Satan, who believes that God is not good, tempted Eve to draw the same conclusion. "Do you really want to gamble," he asked, "that God is good? You have this fruit in your hand. Do you really want to set it aside and run the risk that you'll always wish you had eaten it?"

God claims to love me and have my best interests at heart. Yet sometimes I wonder, like Adam and Eve, *Is God really good, or have I been taken in?* Just when I wish God would rush in and assure me that he certainly does love me and will never do me any harm, God remains intentionally out of reach and out of sight. In his apparent absence, my doubts grow.

It takes little faith to believe in God's existence. One can even obey God without much faith, in the way a slave or a pet obeys a master. Faith enters in at the powerful moments in our lives when we must decide whether or not we believe that God is good.

Faith means stepping onto the path that looks so much like it goes in the wrong direction. I must do this without guarantees, purely because I trust God's assurance that his path will lead to a good place. To follow Jesus' call is counterintuitive, just as abstaining from the fruit of the tree at the center of the Garden was counterintuitive.

When my son was a toddler he fell and had to have stitches put in the wound in his forehead. I had to hold him as the hospital staff swaddled him to a board so he would not move while they put in the stitches. I remember the look of fear and pleading in his eyes as he tried to make sense of his parents allowing such a thing to happen.

I think God sometimes feels like the parent who has to let his children doubt his goodness, knowing that we can't understand what is happening. At such moments we find our greatest temptations to sin.

BENEATH THE CONSCIOUS

The psychoanalyst Ana-Maria Rizzuto wrote of the importance of understanding the difference between our God *concept* and our God image or *representation*. A *representation* is an internalized, largely unconscious experience of another person. We internalize a representation of every person with whom we have a significant relationship. We construct the representation out of our experiences of the person along with our own history, fears, assumptions and guesses. We have internally created a character in the likeness of the person. Since it is our own internal creation, it is limited by our lack of a full experience of the other person and by our inaccurate expectations.

What Rizzuto concluded is that our relationship with God is like our relationships with people. We have a *concept* of the person. We know what we would say if we described that person based on what we consciously think of the person. In addition we have a *representation* of the person, which is much more subtle and intricate and potentially flawed.

I could easily describe to you my concept of my wife. I could tell you about her strengths, her personality quirks, her habits and her weaknesses. Since I know her well, I would present a rather accurate picture of her. At a deeper level, though, I also have a representation of her. Sometimes I expect things from her that are completely out of character. Sometimes I project my own past experiences onto her. My representation of my wife is in the area of intuition and the unconscious, the level not entirely under the influence of conscious concepts.

My God concept includes all that I have studied and learned about God. God is loving, patient, omniscient and perfect. At a deeper level, however, I have an image or representation of God which I am not so quick to share. Sometimes I experience God as distant and aloof. Sometimes I feel he is weak and doesn't seem to be doing a very good job of running the world or managing my life. Sometimes I feel he has failed me, and I feel very angry with him.

To some my words will sound like blasphemy. Once I told an adult Sunday school class about being angry at God. A member of the group grew quite stern with me. Anger at God, he asserted, is a sin. I agreed with him, but I countered that it would also be a sin to lie to God and deny the anger that was actually in my heart.

We do not have much conscious control over our inner images of God or of other people. If I were forced to be away from my wife without contact for an extended time, I would be left with only my inner representation of her. As time went by I would begin to doubt the conclusions I had so confidently formed long ago. I would begin to wonder, *Is she really as good as I remember her to be?* Old fears and doubts would creep in, and I would no longer trust my knowledge of her.

In a similar way, when I am under trials and temptations, I begin to wonder if I am still sure of everything I memorized about God, back when he felt nearer. When faced with a temptation to sin, I may find I have lost confidence in what I used to think God wanted. "Why would

God say no to this? If he would say no to this, he must not be a good God. I need this right now, and God isn't here giving me a better option." We might not say it out loud, but I believe most of us have thought along the same lines when we were faced with a moral choice.

THE MIND OF GOD

The contemplative tradition of Christian spirituality focuses on seeking to know the hidden reaches of the mind of God. It sees knowledge of God at the end of a long search that begins with knowledge of oneself.

John of the Cross articulated the connection between self-knowledge and knowledge of God. He wrote that pain drives us to "self-knowledge, whence, as from a foundation, rises this other knowledge of God. For which cause Saint Augustine said to God: 'Let me know myself, Lord, and I shall know Thee.' For, as the philosophers say, one extreme can be well known by another." The contemplative tradition sees the sequence of awareness going from contemplation of the self, to contemplation of creation, to contemplation of the spiritual realm, to contemplation of God.

Just as a stargazer cleans and calibrates a telescope before looking at the sky, the person seeking to know truth must begin with self-knowledge. The same distortions that affect our view of ourselves and of our world also affect our view of God. I doubt God's goodness because I know that I and those around me are not completely good. I suspect God might enjoy making me squirm because I am capable of enjoying the same kind of power. I suspect that God is distant and unaffected by my pain because I have experienced that from others. Until I become familiar with the distortions of my own perceptions, I cannot even hope to understand God.

In the Eastern Orthodox tradition, spiritual formation revolves around one's battle with *logismoi,* the Greek word for undesirable, sinful thoughts. The concept of *logismoi* is not cognitive; it is not faulty reasoning. *Logismoi* captures the whole of what goes on in a person's heart. *Logismoi* are the passions, desires, fantasies, emotions, wishes, fears, imaginings, longings, revulsions and affective reflexes that are always churning inside us. They must be tamed and brought under submission to the Holy Spirit if we are to attain spiritual maturity.

It is frightening to tackle the passions of the heart. I might manage to get my sinful behaviors under control, but I can't imagine ridding my heart of sinful passions. That is the point of Jesus' emphasis on the heart, and that is its greatest freedom.

The understanding of sin as a disease within the soul, rather than external behaviors, sounds strange to Western ears. We prefer clear and measurable criteria. We want to know if someone committed a sinful act or not; don't trouble us with discussion about what went on in the heart.

I once heard North American culture compared to other cultures through the analogy of football versus soccer. The implicit goal of a soccer game is to keep going without stopping until the end. Flexibility within the rules is often tolerated in the interest of not interrupting the flow of the game. In American football, play consists of brief intense skirmishes, after which everyone stops and progress is minutely measured. If there is any question about a rule being broken, play is suspended and scrutinized on instant replay.

My evangelical faith was thoroughly Western in the way that U.S. football is Western. I was taught to be scrupulous about my behavior. The heart was important only because it could lead me to sinful behavior.

SEVEN SINS

The fourth-century monk Evagrius systematized the traditional understanding of *logismoi* into a list of eight: gluttony, lust, avarice, sadness, anger, acedia, vainglory and pride. In the sixth century Pope Gregory I reduced the list to seven by combining acedia with sadness (which eventually became sloth), combining pride with vainglory, and adding envy. The result was the familiar list of seven deadly sins: *lust, gluttony, greed, sloth, anger, envy* and *pride.*

Many methods have been used to combat the deadly *logismoi*, including physical asceticism and meditation on Scripture passages that focus on each type of thought. Stewart notes that the strongest weapon in the arsenal of the desert fathers and mothers was the practice of radical self-honesty. He quotes Abba Poemen, "Teach your mouth to say that which you have in your heart." The sharing of one's thoughts with another, preferably older and wiser, was expected of everyone in these monastic traditions. The goal was to censor nothing.

The contemporary revival of the art and practice of spiritual direction has brought many ancient ideas to light again. Spiritual direction—otherwise known as *soul friendship* or *soul care*—is the practice of one person vulnerably opening his or her spiritual life to the examination and influence of another.

Christians are increasingly seeking not mere religious education but spiritual formation. We are finding it, not in the contemporary church, but at the feet of contemplative monks from past centuries. As today, the church of that time had become complacent. The first monastics that fled the apostasy of their culture went to the desert to learn to pray and to seek salvation. Pious people came out to them to learn the lessons that their caves and cells had taught them.

Like those ancient believers, I long for holiness. I am not alone; increasing numbers of Christians are looking back beyond what the contemporary church has to offer. We long to rediscover our Christian roots.

Examining our hearts requires courage and humility. It takes courage to face up to our fears; we take the risk of finding out that we are worse sinners than we ever wanted to admit. It takes humility to submit to God's standard rather than our own. Without the courage and humility to start this journey, we will never fully receive the gift of God's grace at the end.

John Wesley reportedly said to one who was neglecting his own spiritual life, "Oh begin! Fix some part of every day for private exercises. . . . Do justice to your own soul; give it time and means to grow: do not starve yourself any longer." With that encouraging word let us explore the most common forms of signature sins.

TAMING YOUR WAYWARD HEART

In each chapter of this book we will explore some questions and exercises to help you take what you have read and apply it to your own spiritual formation. If you don't already keep a journal, you may want to start one in which to jot down your answers to the questions or your experience of the exercises. In the future it will be helpful to go back and review your journal to track your spiritual journey. Feel free to tackle exercises a few at a time rather than plowing through them all at once.

- Think of a time when a friend shared or hinted at a sin, struggle or weakness. How did you respond? (Was your first reflex to respond out of grace or out of judgment?)

  How did it impact your relationship with your friend?

- When you hear of religious or political leaders who sin, what is your initial reaction?

  How would you feel if your pastor publicly confessed his or her sin?

  Do you have stronger reactions to some sins than to others? Why?

- Spend time in silence inviting the Holy Spirit to bring to mind particular sins, patterns of relating and relationships that may need attention. Fifteen minutes of silence is a good starting point from which to grow. For the first few minutes, repeat the following prayer to center your mind and heart: *Lord Jesus Christ, Son of the Living God, have mercy on me, a sinner.* When you have finished, write down what comes to mind. Return to your notes as you read through later chapters of this book.

• Prayerfully reflect on your relationship with God. When you meditate on God, what words, feelings or images come to mind? Don't resist them; just jot them down, whether they seem positive or negative. Be honest with God and yourself.

How would you assess your level of trust in God's goodness right now?

• What are the sins in your life that cling so closely? Consider whether you might actually be fearful about letting them go.

• Abba Poemen said, "Teach your mouth to say that which you have in your heart." What do you consistently harbor in your heart that seems too frightening or impossible to voice?

What do you fear would happen if others began to hear it?

Look for opportunities to disclose those secrets in small ways and in relationships that you trust. Journal about the results. Did your fears come true? Did you find that some people responded better than others?

• Think about how you struggle with fear and pride. If you had to choose, which would you say is a greater struggle for you? Ask a friend that you trust to give you their impression.

As you try to practice greater "radical self-honesty," what are the areas of your heart that are most resistant to being examined? Before you read the next chapter, write them in your journal for later reflection.

2

Pride, Envy, Anger and Gluttony

AS WE SAW IN CHAPTER ONE from earlier lists of sins came the seven deadly sins known to the Western church: *lust, gluttony, greed, sloth, anger, envy* and *pride*. Within these seven basic categories of sin the human heart has the astounding capacity to produce an infinite number of variations.

While it is impossible to list all the names that we could give to human sins, it is worth exploring each of the classic categories of sin and some possible variations of each category. I have especially been helped by a list of subcategories of sin listed in *Saint Augustine's Prayer Book*, a devotional book organized and dedicated to Augustine by the Order of the Holy Cross.

Traditionally the church has taught that God did not create sin *per se*. Sin involves directing something good toward a use that violates God's purpose for it. Church tradition has evaluated sin, especially sinful passions, based on whether the passion is directed toward an appropriate or an inappropriate object of desire and on whether it is expressed in appropriate or inappropriate ways.

A Bus Trip to Heaven

Our signature sins become so familiar to us that we often trust them over the truth. They become so precious to us that we even forget they are sins.

C. S. Lewis wrote an allegory of the struggle between heaven and hell in *The Great Divorce*. In Lewis's fantasy the narrator takes a bus trip from hell to the outskirts of heaven. There he sees the inhabitants of hell, ghostlike people who are not yet fully real, engaged in conversations with the real inhabitants of heaven. One such encounter happens when an angelic being from heaven meets a ghost-man and his companion, a red lizard that lives on his shoulder and both troubles and amuses him with the devilish things it whispers in his ear.

The ghost-man knows he cannot enter heaven with this creature on his shoulder. The angel offers to kill the lizard. At first the man refuses. He fears that if the lizard were killed he would die too. That is the essence of a signature sin, the sin that clings so closely. We come to view it as part of ourselves. We are not sure who we will be without it. We have always believed that it has protected us. Even while we hate it, it is also dear to us.

I have known patients who must grieve the loss of certain areas of sin in their lives. Perhaps their old friend alcohol helped them be the life of the party. Perhaps their extramarital affair awakened them to pleasures they had not known before. I worked with one patient who struggled with an addiction to pornography. As we searched through the history of his addiction, he remembered that he discovered pornography as an adolescent when he lived in an abusive and sexually repressive foster home. The family shamed him so much about sexuality that his discovery of pornography was an escape to a world of greater freedom. Years later he feared that if he promised his wife he would make a complete break from pornography, he might be sucked back into the world of legalism and shame.

The ghost-man in Lewis's story feared the loss of the lizard that was his constant companion. He used many rationalizations to dissuade the angel from killing the lizard. Ultimately he admitted that even if it did kill him to have the sin removed, it would be better than living with the parasite on his shoulder.

The angel killed the lizard and tossed it on the ground. The narrator was shocked when the ghost-man was immediately transformed into a man, real and solid. He was further shocked when the dead lizard was transformed into a beautiful stallion. The man and horse then galloped joyfully up the mountain into heaven. The narrator's guide says, "What is a lizard compared with a stallion? Lust is a poor, weak, whimpering whispering thing compared with that richness and energy of desire which will arise when lust has been killed."

Augustine in particular focused on the ordering of loves. Good things can be loved in inappropriate ways and to the exclusion of more important loves. Our goal is to put our loves in proper order. With this in mind, let us turn to an examination of the major categories of the sins of the human heart.

As you read the following descriptions of the many varieties of sin, be in prayerful reflection about your own signature sins. Take note of those sins that cause a twinge of recognition. Be especially mindful of where you heart may desire *not* to look.

PRIDE: PUTTING GOD ON TRIAL

Pride goes before destruction,
   a haughty spirit before a fall. (Prov 16:18)

Pride is traditionally regarded as the foundational sin. It is understood to be the sin of Satan, expressed in his desire to be like God. Augustine identified pride as the core sin. Pride is most likely to be central in a person's web of signature sins.

Pride wants to put God on trial. One of my adolescent clients was grieving over the many self-destructive things she did during a period of painful depression a year earlier. She expressed a deep desire to feel forgiven for what she had done. She could not fathom receiving forgiveness from God, however, because she felt it was God who had caused all the pain in the first place. Though she was not a prideful person, she demonstrated the elemental struggle of pride: submitting to God's definition of reality rather than our own.

Like a magician using sleight of hand, pride wants to focus attention anywhere but on its own sinfulness: "pay no attention to the man behind the curtain." Pride does not concede that Christ has any authority to condemn our sinfulness. We can be worthy of forgiveness on our own merits. Pride might patronize, but ultimately it refuses to submit.

Pride falls into two types based on whether it is primarily manifested in outward ways or is primarily directed inward.

Outward pride. The outward manifestation of pride shows up in arrogant, haughty and snobbish manners. The outwardly prideful person is oblivious to others and assumes the world should work according to his wishes.

In the Greek myth of Narcissus, a beautiful young man is unmoved by love directed toward him. Because of his self-absorption he is cursed to fall in love with his own reflection in the pond of the lover he spurned, and he dies in this self-absorbed state. The myth explains Freud's use of the term *narcissism* to describe the character disorder of indifference to others. The root of the word *narcissism* is in the Greek word *narkē*, numb. It is also the root of *narcotic*. Numbness to the desires of God and others is characteristic of the signature sin of pride.

Young children go through a period of developmentally appropriate narcissism. An infant or toddler is supposed to feel that she is the center of the world, adored by people who want to be with her. If that need is neglected or disrupted, it becomes solidified into the person's character. If we aren't allowed to feel like the center of the world when we are small, we keep wishing to be the center of the world for years to come. Feeling superior to others is a quick way to satisfy the deeper hunger for a sense of significance.

Thomas Aquinas noted that one kind of pride involves an inordinate desire to excel. The difference between appropriate self-love and the inordinate desire to excel is found in the heart. To want good things for myself is not sinful. To want those good things to the exclusion of better things *is* sinful. Aquinas also noted that the deepest kind of pride is contempt for God—truly desiring to put oneself in God's place. This was the sin of Lucifer. Our selfish ambitions are usually on a smaller scale.

Saint Augustine's Prayer Book lists several forms of pride that are most likely to show on the outside. *Vanity* is a familiar form of pride and takes the form of taking credit for, and boasting about, that which should actually be credited to God. It is an inordinate focus—through time, money or other resources—on one's image. It is an attempt to draw attention to oneself. *Arrogance* is a demanding, overbearing and opinionated form of pride. *Snobbery* is pride over race, family, class or other characteristics that artificially create a sense of superiority. *Irreverence* involves neglect of worship and reverence for God. The irreverently proud person is cynical toward the holy, treats holy things (including God's name) in a profane way or participates in religion purely for social and personal advantage. *Disobedience* shows itself in disregarding God's will and moral laws of morality or in not seeking to understand God's will. *Impenitence* is a form of pride that refuses to seek out and acknowledge one's sin or admit that one has wronged another.

Inward pride. The *inward* manifestation of pride leads a person to be obsessed with others and how they feel about him or her. This person is self-focused, but the person's pride is revealed through inordinate concern with image rather than through arrogant or haughty attitudes. This kind of pride can take the form of "narcissistic humility," gaining praise by acknowledging the smallest faults and feigning brokenness about them. This is a secret pride. The charming and self-effacing person still has the goal of an inflated sense of self.

Secret pride is the most difficult type to combat. Outward sins humiliate us when we realize that everyone can see them, but secret sins flourish in dark corners. For this reason the contemplative traditions of spiritual formation emphasize baring the soul to another person. Pride can only be combated if it is exposed, and secret pride can only be exposed by the one hiding it.

The form of pride in *Saint Augustine's Prayer Book* that is most easily hidden is *distrust*. Distrust involves the rejection of God's will in favor of one's own will. This sin desires to know the future and is unwilling to accept the unknown. Distrust best fits Eve's eating of the fruit in the Garden. Distrust can result in *perfectionism*. A perfectionist may suspect that God's will cannot be accomplished if he or she makes a mistake. Others praise the one who does everything perfectly and always appears perfectly put together. *Sentimentality* is a form of pride when one substitutes pious emotion, pomp and beauty for true private reverence and obedience of God. *Presumption* is another form of pride. Presumption is the distortion of hope, which is one of the classic virtues. It means placing inordinate and disrespectful reliance on self rather than on God's grace. The presumptuous person assumes God will always forgive and makes no attempt to live a life worthy of God's approval.

ENVY: CONSTANT DISCONTENT

> Now Israel loved Joseph more than any of his other sons, because he had been born to him in his old age; and he made a richly ornamented robe for him. When his brothers saw that their father loved him more than any of them, they hated him and could not speak a kind word to him. (Gen 37:3-4)

In popular language the word *envy* is often used as a synonym for *covetousness* or *greed*, but this is not quite accurate. When envy was added as a deadly sin, it was conceived as a spiritually oriented sin, while greed is oriented toward material things. While greed is primarily about possessions, envy is about one's place in the world. Where greed wants the good things that others have, envy wants to be the only one who has good things.

Envy is dissatisfaction with who God has made me to be. It is also suspicion that God is withholding what I deserve and giving it to someone else. When we wish that we were smarter than another or richer than another or more beautiful than another, we succumb to the sin of envy. Envy leads us to become upset at another's success or happiness because envy believes that life is a zero-sum game. If someone else gets something good, there will be less good available for me. Above all, envy is never content.

I once worked with a patient who spent most of our sessions comparing himself unfavorably to others. He didn't bother to find out if the things he imagined about others were true but simply assumed that everyone else was more happy and successful than he was. In one session he shared his fantasies about me and what my life must be like. He painted a picture loosely based on a skeleton of facts he knew about me but richly embellished everywhere else. In his fantasy I had everything that he wished for. That is the essence of envy.

One type of envy particularly strikes parents. We want the best for our children, even better than what we've had. That very situation is fertile ground for envy to take root. I remember times when my son was little and I was providing for him the kind of parenting I wish I had received. I momentarily resented that he had what I wanted. My love for him and my envy momentarily collided, leaving me feeling confused.

I have worked with many people who feel that they received mixed messages from their parents. They received their parents' encouragement to succeed and to explore their gifts and talents. Then when they did succeed and excel, they did not receive their parents' blessing. We can want something for another person and envy the person at the same time.

Envy delights in spoiling what others have. If I can't be happy, envy says, I don't want you to be happy either. Envy thrives in divorce courts. Seemingly normal people turn into green-eyed monsters, trying to make sure that the ex-spouse is left with nothing good after the divorce settlement. Some people spend more money trying to limit what their spouse receives than they stand to lose if they cooperate. They want to make sure their ex-spouse is not happier than they are.

Jealousy is a form of envy that guards what one already has. Jealousy evokes rivalry where none is warranted and imagines competition where none exists. I worked with one couple to try to help them reach an amicable divorce. They were months along in the process but still fighting. The husband made no secret of the fact that he was seriously dating another woman. Nevertheless he flew into a jealous rage one day when he heard from a friend that his soon-to-be ex-wife had been seen at a restaurant with another man. He jealously regarded his wife as his possession and refused to consider the possibility of her belonging to someone else, even though he had already moved on to another woman.

Malice is a form of envy that truly wishes ill for others and delights in observing or contributing to others' pain. One infected with the sin of malice imagines that others have the same secret wishes toward him and that they would similarly cause him pain if they had the chance. Malice is critical, sarcastic, backbiting and bullying. It delights to befriend others with similar tastes, though it will show no loyalty to them and will delight in their pain too if given the chance. Malice led Joseph's brothers to throw him into a pit and sell him into slavery rather than allow him to enjoy his position as favored son.

Contempt is similar to malice. Contempt also seeks violence against another, but in less tangible forms. Contempt takes what is good or neutral and twists it into something bad. The contemptuous person heaps scorn on others' virtues or abilities. It awaits any opportunity to ridicule another, erasing any memory of the other's successes. Contempt takes whatever qualities the contemptuous person does not possess and sullies them so that they do not seem desirable in others. Racism, sexism, classism and all other forms of judging one group of people as superior to another are forms of the sin of contempt.

ANGER: NOT SAFELY TAMED

Better a patient man than a warrior,

a man who controls his temper than one who takes a city.

(Prov 16:32)

The sin of anger or wrath arguably causes more harm in our world than all of the other sins combined. All of the other sins can lead to anger. We easily lose track of the fact that our injured pride came first or that thwarted greed or spurned lust provided a fertile ground for anger to take root. When anger shows up, it often takes over.

Of all of the classic sins, anger receives the most ambivalent reception in a modern audience. The confusion and ambivalence do not come from the assertion that anger can be destructive but from the assertion that anger is always a thought or feeling to be avoided.

We all know that anger can sometimes be good. I would like to be able to say that the historical spiritual formation literature acknowledges anger as a good thing that is sinful only when it gets out of control, but that would not be honest. While inordinate anger is condemned above righteous anger, the centuries-old literature sees anger as a dangerous *logismoi* that should be killed rather than tamed.

John Cassian, who was responsible for bringing much of the teaching and writings of the desert fathers into the broader church, wrote:

The deadly poison of anger has to be utterly rooted out from the inmost corners of our soul. For as long as this remains in our hearts, and blinds with its hurtful darkness the eye of the soul, we can neither acquire right judgment and discretion, nor gain the insight which springs from an honest gaze, or ripeness of counsel, nor can we be partakers of life, or retentive of righteousness, or even have the capacity for spiritual and true light.

Condemnation of such a ubiquitous emotion can be confusing. In several Gospel accounts Jesus himself is angry. He attacked the money-changers who were corrupting the temple. He also seemed quite angry when he confronted the religious leaders. He even seemed angry with his own disciples when they were particularly dense. Some forms of anger must be acceptable.

Traditionally, anger directed at evil that dishonors God is seen as ordinate or appropriate anger. Inordinate or inappropriate anger is directed at selfish and mundane matters. We are justified at being angry only at the evil that also angers God. Unfortunately our motives for anger are seldom pure and untainted by selfishness.

Anger toward people with whom we have close relationships is never simple. There are always old wounds, unresolved tensions and other complications that enter in to the equation. When I think of anger I have felt toward my wife, my son or my colleagues at work, I realize that much more was involved than the issue we were arguing about.

In a recent argument with my wife, I started out feeling completely justified in my anger. As we discussed our points of view, I came to realize that my anger was largely motivated by hurt feelings, embarrassment and a competitive desire to win the argument. There were probably other factors too. Perhaps I had a bad day and took it out on her. Maybe something she said reminded me of something someone else had said or done that made me angry.

Anger at strangers cannot be trusted either. Recently I felt angry with another driver on the road. I was surprised at how quickly my anger flared up over something minor. I had the distinct impression that I had been waiting for an excuse to be angry, and the other driver provided the outlet. I couldn't trust that anger, because it certainly was not righteous indignation.

I must conclude that there is something to the historical warning that anger is not safely tamed. I may raise a bear from a cub so that it becomes relatively safe to be around; however, I would need to stay aware that it still has instincts for aggression, ready to be triggered by the right circumstances. In my day-to-day life I may deal successfully with the normal kinds of anger, but if I turn my back on it at the wrong moment, it will lash out again.

I have known people whose anger is anything but tamed. Theirs is still a wild beast of *rage*, quite easily provoked and overwhelming when awakened. When I work with people who have chronic anger problems, I compare their sin to substance abuse. Alcoholics are not encouraged to try to keep their drinking under control but to abstain from drinking. Alcoholics who try to become social drinkers underestimate the temptations they will face. People who are addicted to rage have a similar struggle. Most people can have an occasional drink and not become alcoholics, and most people can express anger without exploding in a fit of rage. The person with significant anger problems, sometimes trivially called *rage-aholics*, must try to eliminate all anger from their lives. If they invite any anger into their souls, the anger is very difficult to evict.

Resentment is another form of anger that is hard to evict. From a small seed resentment grows into a giant plant with roots entangled throughout our hearts. People who struggle with resentment blame their unhappiness on real or perceived slights and injustices. They refuse to accept God's will or even to accept reality, and they refuse to move on. They build a sense of identity around the injustices inflicted on them. They keep those wounds open rather than letting them heal.

Saint Augustine's Prayer Book lists two other forms of anger: pugnacity and retaliation. *Pugnacity* (what a delightful and descriptive name) is characterized by being combative, quarrelsome or rude. They will see and assume the worst in every situation. The pugnacious person is exhausting to be around, especially if you are the object of the person's pugnacity. If you escape their attacks, their wit can even be amusing, seen from the sidelines. *Retaliation* is a quiet but deadly form of the sin of anger. Like the person with resentment, this person refuses to forgive. Retaliation goes further than resentment, however, and seeks vengeance on those who have done the wrong. People with the sin of retaliation try to subvert others' happiness through active vengeful means or through indirect passive-aggressive means.

To the list of manifestations of the sin of anger, I would add the sin of *paranoia*. Severe paranoia can have medical origins, but it also comes from patterns of the heart. People with paranoid personalities deal with their chronic anxiety by imagining everything that can go wrong and everyone who might wish them ill. This person would rather anticipate the worst and have it not happen than to be caught off guard, unprepared for what life throws at them.

I refuse to be absolute about the admonition to abolish anger. In my experience as a therapist I have seen as many people crippled by their incapacity to experience anger as I have seen people wounded by anger. I have often counseled people to pursue anger, not drive it away. At times anger is not only appropriate but essential for healing. On some occasions it might even be a sin to have no anger at all.

Anger is an appropriate response to evil and injustice. Just as Jesus responded angrily toward those who kept God's children from knowing the love of their Father, we should respond to evil with anger. Unfortunately we are not able to trust our own anger to be like that of Jesus, detached from a self-interested outcome. If my anger cannot come from pure motives, should I try to never feel anger at all? I don't believe that is possible or even desirable. The anger we feel should be proportionate to its object's eternal significance. The evils happening in the Middle East, the AIDS crisis in Africa, the plight of the uninsured in the United States—these things should cause me more anger than the driver who cut me off and almost caused an accident.

I have found ways to determine whether my anger is pure or not. As a spiritual discipline I have to remember to muster up anger about injustice in the world. By contrast the anger about mundane things in my life comes unbidden and in greater intensity than the situation warrants. My selfish anger arises when my desire for control is frustrated. When I get angrier at my uncooperative computer than I do about the drug problem in my community's schools, I know something is wrong.

The ambiguity of anger leaves me with a dilemma. I should be angry about injustice, but not angry in a way that is selfish. For that reason spiritual mentors throughout history have encouraged those under their care to combat all anger in their lives. The passion of anger too easily bursts out from under our control. If we have attained a healthy discipline over our anger, selfish outbursts will be less likely to happen.

Let us add to the list of sinful forms of anger the sin of *obsequiousness*. This sin is characterized by an inordinate rejection of anger and a refusal to take responsible dominion in the world. Some people have been taught that they should never experience anger. Often the message came from those in power who did not want their power threatened. The sin of obsequiousness leads one to passively invest authority in others and to make decisions based on how they might affect relationships rather than on discernment of right and wrong. Obsequious people allow others and even themselves to deny and disrespect the image of God within them. They allow their God-given voice to be silenced.

GLUTTONY: IF A LITTLE IS GOOD, A LOT IS BETTER

> So I commend the enjoyment of life, because nothing is better for a man under the sun than to eat and drink and be glad. Then joy will accompany him in his work all the days of the life God has given him under the sun. (Eccles 8:15)

The sin of gluttony is the pursuit and overindulgence of the body's appetites, especially for food and drink. Care for the physical body, the temple of the Holy Spirit, is an important spiritual discipline.

Gluttony goes beyond healthy self-care. Gluttony believes that if a little is good, a lot will always be better. What makes gluttony a sin is not only the fact that it is bad for the body but that it places the bodily appetites in a superior position to other spiritually good things. Gluttony takes the goodness commended by the writer of Ecclesiastes and makes it into an idol.

Gluttony seeks and becomes addicted to pleasure. In the process pleasure becomes diminished, and it takes greater indulgence to achieve the pleasure that once was sufficient. Gluttony also seeks the easiest route to pleasure. The longer-term pleasures that come from discipline and self-control are more difficult to pursue than the immediately accessible pleasures of food and drink.

I struggle with gluttony. I find it difficult to combat because it begins as something good. Somewhere along the road between taking God-given pleasure in good food and becoming an overweight sedentary person with clogged arteries, I cross a line. Unfortunately I am very poor at discerning that line. One diet club's motto is "nothing tastes as good as being thin," but I have a hard time believing that I'll enjoy future health and fitness as much as I enjoy indulging in delicious foods right now.

During several Lenten seasons I have observed various kinds of fasts. I often have fasted a day a week and given up desserts for the entire six weeks. Each time I do this, I am delighted with the way food begins to take its proper place in my life as a good thing to be enjoyed in moderation. Each time I am also saddened at how quickly I return to my old gluttonous habits. I can discipline myself for six weeks as a gift to God. Somehow I can't bring myself to keep on giving this gift to God and to myself over the long haul.

Gluttony is not only about pleasure. It is also about escape. Pleasure is often used to numb or at least compensate for pain. Though some people stumble into alcoholism or drug addiction while they are just out having a good time, most people who become addicted to a substance have something significant from which they want to hide. The addiction itself heaps on more pain and loss to be faced or escaped, and the cycle worsens. Physical dependency only deepens the problem.

Like alcohol or drugs, food can be a means of escaping from pain. "Eat and drink and be glad," the writer of Ecclesiastes says. When life does not provide you with the rewards you feel you deserve, food is always a reward you can give yourself. Overindulgence in pleasure provides a brief escape from pain. Some foods even boost serotonin and endorphin levels in the brain, like a runner's high, adding fuel to the addictive fire. When the pleasure stops, the pain is still there waiting.

When gluttony is partnered with sloth, health consequences become severe. Diet plans abound, besides the obvious method of eating less and exercising more. A sure way to make fast money is to invent a new easy way to lose weight. Replacing one sin with another, the advertisements for diet plans appeal more to vanity, envy and lust than to the promise of good health.

Sin involves directing something good toward a use which violates God's purpose for it. Gluttony, anger, envy and pride all are classic sins that pervert the good purposes of God our Creator. Next we will examine the sins of lust, greed, sloth and fear.

☙

TAMING YOUR WAYWARD HEART

- As you were reading about pride, what synonym or description stood out for you? What form of pride do you struggle with most?

- Spend a few minutes in listening prayer, asking God to reveal the roots of pride in your life. Write down the thoughts, images or feelings that come to mind.

- Envy is often difficult to admit. Spend some time journaling about ways your heart has wandered into envy. In what ways are you dissatisfied with who God has made you to be?

  What good things do you think that God has withheld from you and given to others?

- What role does anger play in your life? Have you more often been at the giving end or the receiving end of anger? How does that affect your response to facing the sin of anger?

- Spend time in silent contemplation about anger, allowing the Holy Spirit to lead your heart to new awareness.

  What forms of anger come too easily to you?

  What forms of anger might God be calling you to feed rather than avoid?

- Do you struggle with any form of gluttony? What good pleasures do you find most difficult to keep in moderation?

- Do you use food or other pleasures as escape? Spend time in prayer asking God to help you face and deal with the realities that you have been avoiding through gluttony.

- Try taking a fast from the pleasure that most easily grows to excess in your life. How does your heart respond to this discipline? Journal about the effects of your experience.

- As you contemplated each of these sins and its effect on your life, how did you respond to your own wayward heart? Were you harsh and critical, wagging a rebuking finger at yourself? Were you quick to let yourself off the hook, making excuses for your sin? On a continuum from *lax and overly permissive* at one end to *harsh and judgmental* at the other, where would you put yourself?

Would Jesus treat you more like he treated the Pharisees or like he treated the Samaritan woman at the well?

- Do you respond to your own sin differently than you respond to other people's sin? How does this affect your willingness to examine your own signature sins?

3

Lust, Greed, Sloth and Fear

RECENTLY I WAS WATCHING TELEVISION WITH MY SON. An advertisement that we had never seen appeared on the screen. After several wordless seconds of images of billowing clothing, skin and a woman's curves, my son commented, "That must be a car commercial." He was right! Everything from shampoo to fruit is sold with imagery that combines sex and greediness.

The city of Las Vegas built an advertising campaign around the insinuation that there a person can revel in lust without permanent consequences. "What happens here, stays here." In the television ads, vacationers end their time in "sin city" with an ambivalent mixture of embarrassment and enjoyment as they think about what they have just done. This ad campaign is said to have revitalized the Las Vegas economy.

Easy access to pornography has fueled the growth of the Internet. We can bring pornography into our homes at any time of any day. We don't even have to go looking for it. It comes looking for us in unsolicited email and disguised website addresses. Surveys of middle school children show that most of them have accidentally stumbled onto Internet pornography. Hotel chains, video rental stores, and cable, satellite and broadband companies make high profits from pornographic channels and movies.

Lust and greed are natural partners. Sex sells, and advertisers are eager to use it to promote products in popular media.

LUST: THE BROKEN REFLECTION

> When the woman saw that the fruit of the tree was good for food and pleasing to the eye, and also desirable for gaining wisdom, she took some and ate it. She also gave some to her husband, who was with her, and he ate it. (Gen 3:6)

The sexual libido is part of God's good creation. It is also as fallen as any other part of humanity. Sexual sins wound us more deeply than other sins because they strike at the core of the reflection of God's image in us. God created his image-bearers in the form of male and female. Sexuality is meant to be central to our identity and to reflect God's relational nature. Sexuality is at the center of the brokenness of the Fall; therefore it is chief among those aspects of our humanity that need to be redeemed.

Of course lust is nothing new. Humans have always struggled with sexual sins. Among all the sins, the New Testament writers give special emphasis to sexual sins. The difference today is that access to the fodder for lust has never been so readily available and even unavoidable. One would have to be a hermit, avoiding all access to billboards, television, computers, checkout lines, junk mail, newspapers, magazines and pedestrians, to stay free from visual sexual temptation.

Internet pornography is especially addictive. In my work as a therapist I have come to know the power of this secret sin in the lives of many men. The physiological release of endorphins after masturbation, associated with the privacy of using the Internet, combine to create a particular risk of physical and emotional dependency on Internet pornography. Many men lose irretrievable hours and thousands of dollars in an increasingly overpowering whirlpool of shame and secrecy.

Pornography affects the sexes differently, but women are not free from its temptations. Men are more tempted visually, while women are more tempted by fantasies and stories. Pornography contributes to men viewing women as objects, and men who become addicted to pornography tend to have increasing difficulty relating intimately to real women. The pornography trade, along with the advertising industry's objectification of women, holds up idealized physical images of women, contributing to poor self-esteem for women who feel they do not measure up.

I have worked with many women who have been wounded by sexual objectification. Many female patients who were victims of sexual abuse as children are plagued with sexual struggles for years to come. I am especially saddened by stories of girls who became promiscuous in their adolescence and young adulthood. As one woman said, "I felt that I was damaged goods and no decent man would ever be interested in me." Others become fearful of sexuality and avoid intimacy. Still others develop the "lost voice" phenomenon (more on this in chapter seven), and they fall under the power of those who exploit them sexually.

Saint Augustine's Prayer Book includes several forms of the sin of lust. *Unchastity* describes all forms of sexual expression outside of marriage, including unfaithfulness to one's spouse. *Immodesty* involves the attempt to stimulate sexual desire in others or oneself through inappropriate dress, words, actions, images or fantasies. At the opposite extreme, *prudery* is the fear of, or condemnation of, sex and sexuality, including attempts to prevent or repress appropriate discussion and expression of sexuality.

Under "Lust," *Saint Augustine's Prayer Book* includes the interesting category of *cruelty.* Cruelty is the desire to inflict physical or mental pain on others. The lust for power over another person or animal is called *sadism* and is met with the partner sin of *masochism*, the need to submit oneself to pain or humiliation under the power of another.

A man once consulted with me about his struggle with pornography. He had a particular craving for pornography in which one person held power over another and exercised that power in a sexual way. This loving Christian husband and father was mystified about the source of his addiction. We made the connection that his cravings began while he was working under a particularly cruel boss. My patient had been concerned that if he was fired he would not be able to support his family. He felt forced to tolerate his boss's sadistic behavior toward him and other employees. The boss would even require my patient to carry out some of his cruelest abuses on the other employees. It became clear that my patient's desire for sadistic pornography began when he was forced to act out the sadistic fantasies of his boss. With this realization, and the working through of his feelings of anger and humiliation over his boss's behavior, my patient's desire for pornography essentially disappeared.

The sin of lust has its root in the belief that God's love is not enough to satisfy our longing for intimacy. We suspect that God is unfairly withholding from us something that we need. Both the Old and New Testaments use the metaphor of marriage to symbolize our relationship with God. Our sexual drive reflects our inherent desire to be reunited with God. When we pervert and misdirect that desire, we are unfaithful to God, just as Jesus said that a married person who allows lust to thrive in the heart is unfaithful to his or her spouse.

Many single men and women imagine that after they are married they will no longer struggle with lust, only to find after marriage that the struggle continues. Even the most satisfying marital relationship does not completely fill the void that each of us has at our core. Marriage was not meant to satisfy our need for God, only to reflect it. A happy marriage is a tremendous blessing, but only after we abandon the illusion that it will satisfy all our needs.

It is fortunate that we do not have to marry to become spiritually mature, because marriage is not a possibility for some and is unwise for others. In my counseling office I have seen many people who married unwisely. Some gave up their relatively happy single lives based on the illusion that they would not be truly happy until they were married. They only found that the grass was less green on the other side of the fence. Christians with exclusively same-sex attraction, and who believe that the Bible excludes homosexual unions, do not have the option of seeking sexual intimacy. A variety of illnesses and disabilities leave some people incapable of sexual intimacy. Other people are psychologically incapable of the commitment of marriage. Others never meet a suitable mate. Still others choose, as the apostle Paul urged some to do, to forgo marriage so that they could more fully serve in ministry.

For these and other reasons, many people cannot experience sexual union with another person. No one, however, is excused from the responsibility to struggle against the sin of lust. Happily no one is limited in seeking a deeper union with God.

GREED: JUST A LITTLE MORE

> Whoever loves money never has money enough;
>> whoever loves wealth is never satisfied with his income.
>> This too is meaningless. (Eccles 5:10)

> No servant can serve two masters. Either he will hate the one and love the other, or he will be devoted to the one and despise the other. You cannot serve both God and Money. (Lk 16:13)

Greed is lust expressed in nonsexual ways. Greed competes with lust for favored status in American culture. It also competes with anger for the lengths to which we will go to rationalize it as good.

In the movie *Wall Street* the character of corporate raider Gordon Gekko articulates the rationalization of greed. "Greed, for lack of a better word, is good. Greed is right; greed works. Greed clarifies, cuts through, and captures the essence of the evolutionary spirit. Greed, in all of its forms, greed for life, for money, for love, knowledge—has marked the upward surge of mankind." Although the character of Gekko comes to be vilified in the film, his downfall is related less to his greed than to his narcissistic belief that laws and morality do not apply to him.

The topic of money is most likely to start a fight in any marital therapy session. Often one spouse is the spender and the other is the hoarder, at least to their opposing perspectives. Both may struggle with greed, either greed for having or greed for spending. Sometimes their struggle is over how much money to give away; one person may be overly generous and the other overly stingy. Seldom have I worked with a couple who felt they had comfortably resolved their issues with money.

I am carefree with money. My wife is very cautious with it. I like to have money because I want to spend it on pleasurable things. She likes to have money because she wants to save it for an emergency. From our different life experiences each of us has different fears about money.

For more than a decade my wife and I have been part of the same small group. Over the years we have studied and read many things together, but we all agree that some of our most interesting and difficult discussions have been about money.

Several years ago each of us wrote and read to the group our own money autobiography. We found we had an astonishing range of attitudes and experiences about money. We all understood each other much better after the exercise. The married members of the group discovered that other couples' struggles with money were similar to their own.

Anyone who reads the Bible seriously is bound to develop ambivalent feelings about money. Jesus had a lot to say about money and most of it was cautionary. He said that rich people have a harder time entering the kingdom of heaven and that we should be as disinterested in money as the birds and flowers are. He praises the widow who gave her last coin to God, not worrying about what tomorrow would bring.

On the other hand Jesus condemns sloth through the story of a servant who fails to make a profit investing his money for his master. To teach about the Father's love for us, he uses the negative example of a son who is wasteful of his inheritance. He praises the woman who lavished fine perfume on him rather than selling it to feed the poor.

Attitudes toward money and wealth vary widely with culture, family and class. Today I fit in the middle class, but I grew up in a lower socioeconomic status. My attitudes have changed so gradually that I hardly noticed the shift. Things that once seemed like luxuries now feel like necessities.

Social science research has demonstrated that as long as people's basic needs are met, financial status has surprisingly little effect on their sense of well-being. Most people feel that in order to be happy they need just a little bit more than they have. When they get that little bit more, they adjust their standard of living. Then they feel that they need just a little bit more to be happy.

Greed grows out of the suspicion that God will not take care of our needs as well as we can do it ourselves. *Saint Augustine's Prayer Book* has several useful categories of greed or covetousness. *Avarice* is the stereotypical understanding of greed. Avarice is the inordinate pursuit of wealth and material things by either honest or dishonest means. One succumbs to the sin of avarice when one defines worth and success based on material wealth. *Inordinate ambition* captures the lust for power and status. It includes ruthless competition or self-advancement. While such ambition often results in material wealth, the person with the sin of inordinate ambition may regard money as secondary or even irrelevant. Money is useful only as it buys more opportunities. Inordinate ambition may be the most accurate designation for the sin of Lucifer and the sin of Eve.

Prodigality is wastefulness and extravagance. Prodigality describes the sin of the lost son in Jesus' parable. He greedily requested his inheritance in advance so he could use it for extravagant pleasures. We are *prodigal* if we live beyond our means, fail to pay our debts, gamble or spend on unnecessary things for ourselves while others go without what they need. The line between need and want is difficult to identify. Some would argue that my air conditioner is an extravagance and that I should have given that money to feed the poor. Others would argue that as long as I tithe, I can spend the rest of my money as I wish. Others have different standards, and some don't entertain the question at all; we will discuss that under the sin of sloth. I believe that pursuit of pleasure and comfort at the expense of the natural environment also fits into the category of prodigality. We are to be stewards of creation, not consumers of it.

Saint Augustine's Prayer Book puts *penuriousness* at the opposite end of the spectrum. We would use the term *stinginess*. This is the sin of Scrooge who inordinately hoarded his money. When we are obsessed with security and imagine that wealth can protect us, we commit the sin of stinginess. As Jesus' parable of the rich fool tells us, we may hoard our riches but lose our souls. Taking advantage of others or refusing to be generous to others are evidence of penuriousness. So is failure to tithe our income and our talents. As Jesus said, "From everyone who has been given much, much will be demanded; and from the one who has been entrusted with much, much more will be asked" (Lk 12:48).

Finally the sin of *domination* fits under greed. We commit this sin when we insist on having things our own way. Some people crave domination so much they will do anything to get it, even sabotage their own goals and drive others away. The dominant person is often skilled at appearing to have others' best interests at heart while he presumes to know what is best for them. This person gives and helps, but with strings attached.

We commit the sin of domination when we influence others toward sin or impose our will on others by force, manipulation or passive-aggressiveness. I watched a woman in a store exercising domination over the salesperson who had to follow her around the store, listening to her prattling on, fulfilling her every whim. She was using the carrot of her eventual purchase, and possibly the power of knowing that the clerk was required to please the customer, to exercise dominance as if the salesperson were her personal servant.

Sloth: The Reverse of Worship

> I know your deeds, that you are neither cold nor hot. I wish you
> were either one or the other! So, because you are lukewarm—
> neither hot nor cold—I am about to spit you out of my mouth.
> You say, 'I am rich; I have acquired wealth and do not need a
> thing.' But you do not realize that you are wretched, pitiful, poor,
> blind and naked. (Rev 3:15-17)

Sloth has come to be synonymous with physical laziness, but the original Greek word *akēdia* has a rather different meaning. *Acedia* is spiritual listlessness or laziness. It is the antithesis of worship. Sloth is the neglect of the greatest commandment: to love the lord your God with all your heart, soul, mind and strength.

The purpose of this book is to counter the sin of sloth. We are slothful when we do not attend to our spiritual lives. We are slothful when we neglect anything that God asks of us and when we don't do what needs to be done.

Jonah was slothful when he refused to go to Nineveh. Moses was slothful when he resisted God's command to go and speak to Pharaoh. Peter was slothful when he tried to talk Jesus out of submitting to his destiny of dying on the cross. The disciples were slothful when they fell asleep in the garden of Gethsemane.

I am slothful when I watch one more TV show when I should read a book, or when I sleep a few extra minutes when I promised myself I would get up to pray or exercise. Depending on the context and one's temperament, sloth can look like cowardice, idleness, apathy, contentment, gullibility, stubbornness, unimaginativeness, boredom, rigidity, restlessness or complacency.

When I lead retreats or discussions on the topic of sin, people have often expressed frustration: they want to talk about more positive topics and avoid the morbid and depressing realities. Some have distanced themselves from the worm theology of their religious upbringing, where they were tormented with a constant sense of doom and gloom. The pendulum swings to extremes. Hypervigilance about sin is oppressive and shaming; but in response, many people retreat to the contrasting sin of spiritual sloth and neglect to examine their hearts for sin.

The neglect of spiritual formation is a sin of slothfulness. Many Christians have a "just do it" mentality about their spiritual lives. "If we just get our behavior under control so we are not sinning outwardly, we have success. Then we can forget about ourselves and get to the work of saving the world." I doubt that I ever heard those precise words, but it was the philosophy I internalized while growing up in an evangelical church. I was not taught what I now believe, that spiritual formation is a lifelong journey of being gradually transformed into the image of Christ. It is not a once-and-for-all event. In the old model the spiritual life was like joining the military. You get sent to boot camp where you are taught all you need to know to be a soldier. Then you are sent out onto the battlefield to do the real work. The quicker you learn, the better. The faster you can give up milk and move on to meat, the more spiritually successful you are.

The just-do-it model of spiritual life had a comforting simplicity. It felt good to think I could actually accomplish spiritual maturity and become sanctified. Although it had a clean and orderly feel, I wouldn't go back to that way of thinking and miss out on the richness of a continuing spiritual pilgrimage.

I now see that the just-do-it message is mired in the sin of sloth. Sloth comes from distrust that God's goodness is sufficient to make the hard work of the spiritual life bear fruit. By declaring that our own house is in order and focusing on what others are doing wrong, we neglect our own spiritual formation and lose an opportunity to grow more fully into the image of Christ.

Sloth also takes the form of refusing to receive and to give grace. The Pharisees were slothful in this sense. It is easier to check off a list of behaviors than to look into one's heart and sweep out the corners. If I were a Pharisee who had spent my life getting every tiny detail of every day just right, I wouldn't want to hear Jesus' message that it had all been a complete waste. I would want to keep everything just as it was.

Saint Augustine's Prayer Book describes the sin of sloth as "the refusal to respond to our opportunities for growth, service or sacrifice" and lists two types of this sin: *laziness* and *indifference*.

Laziness takes in all forms of neglect of our responsibilities to family, employer, society, church and any other area of life. It can mean focusing only on the more pleasant and enjoyable tasks and leaving the others to someone else. Superficial busyness and triviality are manifestations of sloth; so are an inordinate focus on rest, recreation and pleasure. In the life of the monk, sloth was the neglect of spiritual duties. Since the lives of monks revolved around a strenuous schedule of worship and prayer, spiritual laziness could be tied to physical laziness.

Indifference is lack of concern about injustice. Another word for it is *apathy*. Sloth shows itself in a deliberate lack of awareness or an attempt to escape from the realities of suffering in the world. Neglect of the responsibility to stay informed about contemporary issues is the sin of indifference. Refusal to minister to the needs of those around us is also indifference. Finally, seeing the church as a place of social participation rather than a place of worship and spiritual transformation is a rampant expression of the sin of indifference.

Cowardice is another form of sloth. The coward uses the risk of something painful or unpleasant as an excuse to refuse to do what is necessary. Here is an example of disordered loves. We see our own comfort and safety as more important than justice. Has God called you to serve in a homeless shelter? Cowardice would let your fear of an unfamiliar neighborhood keep you from obeying. Has God called you to speak out against sin? Cowardice would keep you at home minding your own business.

SADNESS: MISTAKEN IDENTITY

I will add *sadness* under the sin of sloth because sadness was originally included in Evagrius's list of eight *logismoi*. When sadness and acedia were combined into the sin of sloth, sadness became lost in the descriptions of the deadly sins.

Sadness is difficult to regard as a sin. Sadness usually exists because of legitimate losses. Early descriptions of sin as sadness fit what we might call *morbidity* or *despair*. The one who engages in a sinful sadness savors and takes pleasure in being sad. Unlike the sadness associated with mourning, this sadness is not productive and does not promote healing from a loss.

I have worked with people who struggle with sadness. They have built an identity around being sad and resist the things that would normally bring someone out of sadness. They refuse to do the healing work of mourning and move on. They can even enjoy the power they feel when they frustrate others with their pessimism. They suspect that if they begin to feel happy, their hopes will be dashed; therefore it is best not to take the risk.

Self-examination is difficult and painful. It should not be morbid, but it should also not be neglected. Sloth is overcome by trust that God wants to do something in our lives that will more than compensate for the pain and work required to reach that end.

FEAR: SOMETIMES A VIRTUE

> There is no fear in love. But perfect love drives out fear, because fear has to do with punishment. The one who fears is not made perfect in love. (I Jn 4:18)

Although fear is obviously a potential source of sin, it does not appear in any of the traditional lists of the capital sins, those from which other sins spring. To my knowledge fear is never listed as a subcategory of any other sin. Aquinas considered hope and fear to be two passions that do not easily fit into the classic list of seven deadly sins.

Hope is primarily a virtue but is sometimes a sin. Fear is primarily a sin but is sometimes a virtue. Earlier we looked at presumption, the sinful form of hope, as a type of pride. Cowardice is included as a form of sloth. Sadness or despair, a kind of fear, is also part sloth. But fear itself doesn't fit clearly anywhere in the list of sins.

Aquinas resolved the problem by categorizing fear according to which of the other sins describes its source or its object. For example, the fear that God will not provide for our needs can lead to the sin of greed. The fear that spiritual growth will be painful can lead to the sin of sloth.

Throughout the preceding chapters I have explored Oswald Chambers's idea that all sin stems from the suspicion that God is not good. In that sense all sin stems from fear. We sin because we fear that we cannot trust God. The form of our fear defines the particular sin that we employ to avoid the object of fear.

Fear leads us to deny the suffering of Jesus and to want to skip over our own or anyone else's suffering as well. Fear lives by hiding from the truth.

Perhaps you know someone who simply gives up when confronted, rather than puts up an appropriate resistance. People who are controlled by fear hope to earn approval by being whatever others want them to be. Those controlled by fear do not want to examine their lives for sin because they are terrified at what they might find. Ignorance is bliss, they say; what I don't know can't hurt me. Their desire is to escape off to heaven without having to deal with the messiness of earth.

Fear is confusing because it can also be a virtue. We are commanded to fear the Lord. Aquinas identified several levels of maturity in what he called the gift of fear, given to us by the Holy Spirit.

Servile fear is the least mature; it is neither a sin nor a virtue. Servile fear describes every mortal's dread of being punished. The prodigal son eventually came back to his father because of servile fear; he would starve if he didn't repent. Obedience out of servile fear is basically good but not exceptionally honoring to God.

Initial fear is the next level of maturity of the Holy Spirit's gift of fear. Like the prodigal son's older brother, initial fear obeys because it is right to obey. There is some fear of punishment but also a desire to be obedient.

Finally, *filial fear* was regarded as the most mature level of Spirit-given fear. Otherwise called *reverential fear*, it is motivated by a true love of God. Filial fear flees from sin because sin is displeasing to God. The father of the prodigal son illustrates this level of maturity. His love is pure and unselfish.

All other fear that does not fit into the fear of the Lord, Aquinas and other early writers called *mundane fear*. It is neither a sin nor a virtue. It is simply a rational reaction to danger. It does not have moral implications unless it becomes inordinate and starts to control the person.

Whether a sin, a virtue or mundane, fear cannot be simply dismissed. Fear is so centrally involved in all of the sins that I believe it deserves separate discussion. I have known several people who came to name *fear* as their signature sin.

Sometimes a person struggles with a particular type of fear that is best accounted for by another sin. If I am principally afraid that I will come to poverty, I will likely struggle with the sin of greed.

But what if a person struggles with fear itself, many kinds of fear in a wide variety of situations? What if fear truly rules their lives?

Fear has plagued humanity ever since the Fall. After Adam and Eve sinned they hid themselves from God in the Garden. When God called out for Adam, he answered, "I heard you in the garden, and I was afraid because I was naked; so I hid" (Gen 3:10). Adam's first response after sinning was the *initial fear* of God. Adam's and Eve's eyes had been opened to good and evil, yet they were not prepared to handle their own awareness.

I haven't counted, but I have heard that the most common directive in the Bible is "Do not be afraid." Often the reassurance is given to people facing painful and dangerous circumstances. How can we be asked not to fear danger? Aquinas's answer is that, like any passion, fear that is inordinate is sinful, while fear that is in order is not sinful. Fear of an approaching bear is in order. Fear that God will not show his love for me is not.

Fear is a sin when it should be dispelled by our experience of God. After the exodus from Egypt, when the Israelites came to the border of the promised land, they did not enter it because they were afraid of the people who inhabited it. After everything God had done for them, they still did not trust his word when he told them he would deliver the land into their hands. Their sinful fear sent them back into the desert for forty years.

I have worked with several couples whose marriages have been scarred by infidelity. Often the betrayed spouse suffers from fears of repeated infidelity. It is usually a reasonable fear. In some cases, however, the offending spouse has done everything possible to repent and prove himself or herself worthy of renewed trust. Years later the offending spouse is still being punished for a past indiscretion. In one case the wife was still raking her husband over the coals for a brief emotional affair he had twenty-five years earlier.

Our trust in God should not require constant proof. God patiently shows himself to be our loving Father. At some point our faith should grow up enough to need less proof of his faithfulness.

Human creativity, a part of the *imago Dei*, is expressed in the countless ways we find to protect ourselves and resist the will of God. We have explored the major categories of sin with some variations within each category. Anyone on a pilgrimage toward deeper spiritual formation, however, must move beyond acquaintance with the definitions of sin. We must examine our own hearts and name the unique patterns that sin has etched in our souls. For this reason let us turn to a discussion of the process of naming our own signature sins.

6

TAMING YOUR WAYWARD HEART

- Of the many variations on the sin of lust, which one most readily tempts your wayward heart? How has your personal struggle with lust been influenced by painful experiences and relationships in your life?

- Carry a journal with you over the course of several days. Keep a record of times when you struggle with lustful thoughts, desires or fantasies.

    Do you notice any consistent patterns?

    Are you more tempted at some times than others?

    Do some images disappear more quickly than others?

    Prayerfully consider how to make concrete changes in your life to re-move temptations to lust or to lessen the impact of those temptations.

- When the heart has wandered too long in lust, we may need another person's help to escape from it. Prayerfully consider whether you need an accountability partner and/or professional help in combating this sin or seeking healing for past wounds.

- Do questions about money make you feel defensive?

    Do you feel more or less wealthy than your neighbors?

    Than most people in the world?

    Prayerfully submit to the Lord your heart's attitudes toward money.

- Do you struggle with any form of greed?

    How do you feel God calling you to address it?

- Write your own money autobiography. How did your parents handle money? How were discussions about money handled or avoided?

    If you are married, how do your attitudes about money differ from your spouse? How do you feel God wants your views of money to change over time?

- If you are reading this book and answering these questions, you are combating sloth!

    What most easily tempts you toward sloth?

    What are your most common excuses for not doing the important things that need to be done?

- Worship is the antithesis of sloth. What hinders your ability to worship?

    Following the next worship service that you attend, journal about the experience. How did your mood affect it?

    What factors distracted you?

    What factors drew you in and made worship more natural?

    Were you more concerned with what you wanted from the worship experience or with what God might desire from your worship? How does this relate to the sin of sloth?

- In what ways does fear keep you from becoming the person God created you to be? If God healed you from the sin of fear, what would dramatically change in your life?

- As in the previous chapter, when you contemplated each of the sins in this chapter and its effect on your life, how did you respond to your own wayward heart? Were you harsh and critical, or were you gentle and patient?

4

Naming Our Signature Sins

YEARS AGO I BEGAN TO STUDY THE HISTORY and writings of Christian contemplative spirituality, particularly the sayings of the desert fathers and mothers. I had a deep longing for the transformation of heart that was evident in the lives of those who engaged in contemplative practice.

I felt the Holy Spirit calling me to begin to address the areas of sin discussed in the previous chapters. The roots of these sins have gone down deep. I imagined a web of sins crisscrossing and intertwining with every part of my soul. These sins sought to insinuate themselves into every good part of my self, choking off what they could, hampering the growth of what they could not kill.

Though such a web of sin sounds overwhelming and hopeless to combat, I believe that there are nexus points where we can effectively fight it. The tendrils of every root system extend from a central point. Just as our patterns of sin are unique, the places where sin has most taken root are somewhat different for each person. I have found it helpful, for myself and for those who have sought my counsel, to seek out the one primary root of sin which lies at the core. The central root will be an old familiar nemesis. Its name is often known but seldom spoken.

The signature sin at the center of my own personal web is pride. It may not sound profound to admit that I struggle with the father of all sins. The first sin, the sin of Lucifer, is said to be at the heart of every sin committed. Where is the uniqueness in that?

Yet when I say that my signature sin is the sin of pride, it conjures images for me. I see the unique ways that pride infects my day. I see the ways that I try to impress others. I see the ways I seek admiration from others. I see the jokes I make at a meeting to insert myself into every discussion. I see the ways I try to escape responsibility for my mistakes. I see the internal wheels turning right now, wondering if people will be impressed with my honesty.

THE POWER OF NAMING

I have a common first name, Michael. I know several other Michaels. When I think of them or say hello to them, however, their name does not seem as familiar as when I introduce myself with "Hello, my name is Michael." When we name something it becomes unique in our minds in a significant way. More is attached to that name than its letters and syllables. All of my experiences with that thing or that person are connected to it. My feelings and images about a person come immediately to the surface when I speak the person's name.

In a similar way, when I speak of my signature sin of pride I mean something entirely different than when I speak of the universal sin of pride. My pride is unique, like my signature or my fingerprint. I don't struggle with the same forms of pride as another person. I don't struggle with pride at the same times as another person. My pride, like my shadow, is shaped exactly like me.

When I speak of naming our signature sins, I am referring to the intimate task of "knowing" one's secret nemesis. For some the naming is quick and obvious because we are very familiar with this sin. I knew immediately that my most central sin was pride.

Often the naming is more difficult. My wife eventually named fear as her central sin. Though the outline of the sin was clear to her, its name was not clear. Fear does not seem like a sin, and normally it is not. For my wife, however, *fear* captured an image of the roots that sink themselves into her heart and the ways that fear threatens and tempts her from being the woman God wants her to be.

When we seek to name our signature sins, we should enter the process with reverence and prayer. Whether we identify the name quickly or take a significant amount of time to uncover it, accuracy and thoroughness should be our first priority. When the sin is named, we have taken a greater level of ownership for it. The naming of the signature sin is the most important step in conquering it.

I am one of the few members of my family of origin who goes by my given name. Most of the others go by their middle names. I know several people who are known by a name that does not even appear on their birth certificate. There is always a story behind the name change. Sometimes a new name marks a significant alternation from the "old me" to a new identity, as when God renamed Jacob as Israel or Saul as Paul.

We should take great care when we name our signature sins. The process of choosing a name requires a growing familiarity with the sin itself. Any word chosen will carry subtle shades of meaning.

Think of the differences between the words pride, vanity, entitlement, arrogance, self-love, self-focus, selfishness, self-absorption, self-centeredness, impenitence, snobbery, grandiosity, conceit and narcissism. Each name evokes subtly or significantly different images. If we hastily latch onto to a name for the sin we are uncovering, we might learn later that it no longer fits. We should take things slowly and should prayerfully submit to God's naming of our sin.

DOWN TO EARTH

The maxim "Know Thyself" was inscribed above the door of the ancient Greek temple of Apollo. The phrase was so widespread that its origin has been attributed to several different philosophers. The aphorism has been used to justify many kinds of self-absorption, but its central truth is biblical. In both the Old and New Testaments God consistently calls his people to have pure hearts turned toward him. This quest is made difficult by our natural fallen ambivalence; we simultaneously long for and shrink from self-knowledge. Our deceptive hearts must be plumbed if we are to turn them over to God.

The word "humble" has its root in *humus*, meaning soil or ground. Humility is often misconstrued as having a lowly view of oneself, down in the dirt. Humility is better understood as being down to earth, grounded in reality. The goal of maturity is an entirely accurate view of oneself with no distortions or inaccuracies. For many people humility requires a step down in their perception of themselves. Others must take a step up in their view of themselves to attain an accurate—and therefore humble—self-perception.

It is virtually impossible to attain humility if we are left to our own devices. It is like picking out our own eyeglass frames. I have severe astigmatism. Without corrective lenses I see very poorly. When I go to buy new glasses, I am faced with the dilemma of trying to choose attractive frames when I can't see how they look on my face. I must take along someone I trust to tell me which frames look best on me.

How can I find and correct the distortions in my view of myself and of the world by looking through the same lenses that cause the distortions in the first place? Another person must stand beside me while I describe what I see. That person can then point out any slight (or severe) deformities in my vision.

The ancient and contemporary practice of spiritual direction involves allowing a trusted person close enough to help us grow deeper in our relationship with God. We let this person point out the flaws in the lenses of our hearts.

Spiritual direction was once a common practice for those entering religious orders or professions. The spiritual director had the task of ridding the directee of worldliness.

To postmodern sensibilities such vulnerable submission to the authority of another seems intolerable. Despite our culture's distrust of spiritual authority, the role of spiritual friend, guide, mentor or director is enjoying a renaissance. Training programs in spiritual direction have sprung up all around the country, merging the ancient practice of spiritual direction with modern concepts of professional counseling. Although a certificate in spiritual direction can never guarantee sufficient spiritual maturity to guide others' souls, Western spirituality has become so individualistic that we should welcome the trend back to seeking authority outside of the self.

The Protestant Reformation brought recognition of each person's right to confess sins directly to God. In the process, however, the confessional was lost. For Protestants the Reformation did away with an important opportunity for exercising personal spiritual direction between priest and parishioner.

The psychotherapy professions have inappropriately become the postmodern equivalent of the confessional. The problem is that they lack any corresponding moral foundation for handling people's confessions. The church is reawakening to its responsibility to provide a place for confession through spiritual direction. The move is a welcome corrective to relativistic psychotherapy.

As a psychotherapist I believe in the process of psychological healing and its role in spiritual healing. I often encourage my patients to seek out a spiritual director or mentor to help them translate their healing into a more meaningful life with God. It is important, however, to know the distinction between therapy and spiritual direction, despite their areas of overlap.

Psychotherapy may range across many areas of problems in a person's relational life, some of which affect their spiritual life. Spiritual direction remains primarily focused on deepening one's relationship with God, even though it may involve discussion of other issues.

A SPIRITUAL FRIEND

The quest for spiritual humility is not for the faint-hearted. We should not enter into it alone. Every believer should have at least one spiritual friend or mentor who helps him or her draw closer to God. For some that person is their pastor; however, many pastors lack the necessary gifts to be effective spiritual directors. Even those blessed with such gifts cannot meet the spiritual direction needs of every person in the congregation. In most churches wise and discerning believers are untapped and unappreciated treasures for spiritual direction.

Once we find the courage to stand before others without our masks of image management, we can see in their response to us who we really are. With their help we can examine and name the sins that cling so closely. In naming and examining them half our battle is won.

Once we have settled on a name for our signature sin, what do we do? How do we do battle with it? How do we seek to have our needs met in healthy ways so we may give up our signature sin? No matter how we ask the question, the answer is the same. We can do little to help ourselves in this realm; we must turn ourselves over to God.

Like all of our spiritual formation, we exercise little control over the outcome; we can do little to rid ourselves of these deceptive layers of sin. The force of our own wills may take us a step or two, but no farther. What we can do is willingly surrender to the Holy Spirit's scalpel.

One of C. S. Lewis's Narnia Chronicles, *The Voyage of the "Dawn Treader,"* has a striking Christian metaphor for submitting to God's painful but healing transformation. Eustace Scrubb undergoes an agonizing but freeing transformation as Aslan removes his layers of dragon's scales. Anyone who submits to such an undressing, such a purging of sin, will be smaller and humbler when the process is completed. To be made into a new creature is both painful and profoundly liberating.

Aslan miraculously stripped away Eustace's layers of dragon skin. Sometimes God works such transformative miracles in our lives. The pain may be exquisite but it is over quickly. Often God chooses to use a longer and slower process of spiritual transformation.

Something so deeply rooted and pervasive as a signature sin seldom submits to a once-for-always change. Like Paul's thorn in the flesh, we must usually wrestle with that sin for the rest of our lives. If my task were combating sin in general, I would be overwhelmed. My task, however, is to combat *my* sin. I am not facing some unknown distant adversary. This is *my* signature—uniquely mine. I do not have to go out on a quest in search of it. Once I have named my sin, I know where it is, always. It is right there in my heart.

THE NAIL ON THE DECK

I picture my signature sin as a protruding nail on my deck. With time and weather and repeated foot traffic it works its way above the surface. When I want to keep it from tripping me, I do not need to waste my time scouring the surface of the deck to find it. I know exactly where that nail is. With my hammer I can drive it down with one stroke.

Prayer is the hammer that drives down the offending nail. When I remodeled our kitchen I used a hammer in many different ways. In the demolition phase it made a great weapon for breaking plaster and lath, and I enjoyed its destructive power. If I wanted to tear apart a wall I could swing my hammer indiscriminately. When it came time to build up rather than tear down, I needed to use my hammer in a different way. To put up a wall, I needed to carefully aim the hammer. The skill was in being able to aim it at exactly the right spot and keep my thumb out of the way. In the beginning I missed many nails and had to waste time patching holes. With practice, I could use my hammer accurately and efficiently.

Imagine a blindfolded carpenter. What a useless waste of time! Confessing and combating the whole spectrum of sin is as inefficient as trying to remodel a kitchen while wearing a blindfold. Why grope around in the dark? Why go into the process with the assumption that I have to scour every area of my life for any manner of random sin? I know where the nails consistently poke out. If I take off the blindfold, I can see the nail I am driving and can hit it quite accurately.

When I confess my sins to God, I do not need to flail around wondering what they are. I find that they are lurking in the same places in my life where I found them yesterday and every day before.

When I first began to take seriously the purgative task of naming my signature sin, I felt led by the Holy Spirit to commit myself to confessing my signature sin of pride every time I went to the Lord in prayer. I began every session of prayer with a simple confession, "Forgive my pride," and a simple request, "Teach me humility." Every time I prayed, whether once a day or multiple times, I asked God to forgive my pride. I would pause then as the Holy Spirit revealed the tendrils of the sin of pride in my life.

The old saying "Be careful what you pray for" came to mind as I prayed that prayer dozens, then hundreds of times. God began to strip away the illusions I had constructed to hide my sin from myself. I have a short attention span for looking at my own sin; but I had made a covenant, and for a period of several months the Holy Spirit did not let me forget my promise. My short attention span was no excuse. My promise was too simple.

Over and over my sin of pride was brought before my eyes. Even in corners where I thought there was no sin, I found its tendrils. It was a very painful time, but I still remember it with tremendous fondness. Layers of dragon skin came off, not one at a time, but in sheets. All my life I had hidden from the simple truth of my pride. Hiding it had consumed massive amounts of my energy and creativity. Because I carefully hid my sin, I had not let anyone else close enough to see it, and so there was no one to help me rid myself of it. Only the persistent daily confession of my sin allowed God to peel it away.

Jesus told a parable of a widow who pestered a judge to bring her justice (Lk 18:1-8). Though the judge was not a godly man, he relented so the woman would cease her pleas. Jesus says that we should be as relentless with God as the widow was with the judge.

Perhaps through our persistence God measures the desires of our hearts. Like all children, when my son was small he would notice something in a store that caught his fancy. When he asked for it we sometimes answered, "If you remind us next week about that toy we will come back and buy it then." Usually he forgot about it. If he remembered, we were happy to buy it for him. We knew it was truly a desire of his heart.

If we confess our sin and ask God's forgiveness with the persistence of the widow in Jesus' parable, we will affirm to God that the true desire of our hearts is to be purged of our sin. God delights in giving us the desires of our hearts. Like a good parent, he does not give us every trivial thing we request. Nor does he always give us the important things that we treat trivially in our prayers. What God wants is not for me to merely confess my sin of pride; he already knows about it. He wants a change in my heart.

After his victory over the Amalekites, King Saul arrogantly disobeyed God's command to destroy all their livestock. When the prophet Samuel confronted him, Saul countered that he should be excused from obeying the commandment literally because he had saved the best livestock to present as a sacrifice to God. Samuel countered, "To obey is better than sacrifice, and to heed is better than the fat of rams" (1 Sam 15:22).

God does not want words and liturgies if our conduct proves them hollow. Empty confessions do not hide our guilty hearts from God any more than the bushes in the Garden hid guilt-ridden Adam and Eve.

THE HEART IS FORGETFUL

The prophet Jeremiah proclaimed, "The heart is deceitful above all things / and beyond cure. / Who can understand it?" (Jer 17:9). Nowhere is self-deception more evident than in the confession of sin.

After I named pride as my signature sin, with the leading of the Holy Spirit I gradually named several other offshoot sins. They are all written in my journal. However, as I write this, I cannot remember exactly how many of them are on the list without looking at it. In fact I've been out of the habit of naming the entire list for a while, and I can't remember the last couple of sins on the list at all.

Just as you can follow a root from the soil surface down to the tendrils at the greater depths, you can follow the web of a signature sin to the depths of the heart. My heart does not want to face my sin. It would rather forget my sin entirely.

As the apostle Paul shows in Romans 7, there is a war within my inner being. The renewed part of me wants to obey God and rid my life of sin. My broken unregenerate self fights against such submission. I secretly suspect that God might not have my best interests at heart, that God might not be good.

I have worked with families who intervene to confront the sin of one family member. Once the confronted person acknowledges the sin, the rest of the family wants to be done with the issue forever and never speak of it again. Later the offender repeats the sin. Dumbfounded, the family asks how it could have happened again.

Love does not leave another person to face temptation alone. Love consistently supports the sinner and holds the person accountable. If I love myself as God loves me, I must do the same. I must hold my heart always accountable and submit its most vulnerable corners to God's persistent weeding.

Immediately after we face, name and confess our signature sin, the first reaction is mourning. We must admit that we are not who we pretended to be. We must also mourn the lost years, the lost relationships and the lost opportunities that our sin has stolen from us. Though our sins are repugnant, we are not quite sure who we will be without them. We do not know what others will think of us now.

Despite a sense of mourning, I discovered that I felt like a victim of long-term blackmail who has suddenly decided to reveal the incriminating evidence rather than continue under the oppressive power of the blackmailer. If I revealed it myself, I had no reason to fear that it might accidentally be uncovered, exposing me as an imposter. Once I named and owned my sin, it held less power over me.

MEETING GOD AT BOTH POLES

The most intimate and profound encounters with God are two-sided. On the one hand, an encounter with God exposes our unworthiness and the deep sin both of ourselves and of all the human race. On the other hand, an encounter with God reveals the astounding reality that his grace is sufficient to cover all the wickedness that ever has existed or ever will exist. The incomprehensible paradox of law and grace permeates everything.

When we encounter God we experience the bipolar ambivalence of shame at our sin coupled with unbridled joy at God's forgiveness. I do not trust my own or others' religious experiences if they are characterized by only one of the two poles. I can be wrong, but I have known too many believers who are crippled by guilt and shame and unable or unwilling to receive God's grace. Likewise I have heard too many descriptions of worship or prayer encounters that were only pleasurable with no corresponding experience of being "undone" by the overshadowing presence of God's holiness.

I enjoy most contemporary Christian praise music, but I find that some songs have a superficial, hypomanic character. God is not a safe teddy bear to be carried around for comfort. Reverence and fear of the

Lord should never be sacrificed for a safe and cozy Jesus. God's mercy is equally important, however, to keep us from drowning in the painful awareness of our inability to hit the mark. Each time I come face to face with my sin and the fact that I have failed for the millionth time to measure up to what God expects of me, I mourn my sin. Each time I confess my sin to God and receive his loving forgiveness, I rejoice in his goodness and grace.

Mourning is an essential and natural response to sin. Unwillingness to mourn is a deadly malady of the soul. Mourning is a healthy process by which a person heals from the wound of a loss of some kind. In the healing process the person comes to terms with the loss, whether a lost relationship, a lost innocence or a lost dream. In accepting and healing the loss, the person emerges ready to move on to other relationships, a more mature reality or a new dream.

Mourning is not the same as depression. Freud aptly observed that *melancholia*, as depression was once called, is characterized by unwillingness or inability to mourn. Melancholic people curl up in a ball and try to pretend that the loss has not taken place. They cling to the fantasy that the object of their love—whether person, illusion or dream—is still there. They become numb, and their field of vision becomes very small. Their tears are empty and unsatisfying. The person who defends melancholia is afraid to hope that there might be something new out there that could take the place of the precious object of attachment. If they stand up and look around they will see the empty place where it once was and acknowledge that it is time to move on without the treasured object.

No one likes to mourn. We were not created with mourning in mind. The painful acknowledgment of any loss is an aching reminder that things are not the way they are supposed to be. We were created for eternity with God, where nothing good is ever lost. The human heart is constantly tempted to live under the illusion that things are fine just the way they are.

Naming and owning up to my sin forces me to look reality square in the face. My heart longs for eternity with God, but I live far from that home.

ACTING THE PART

At a remarkably young age, children begin to try to cover up their transgressions. Like Adam and Eve, their first instinct after committing a sin is to hide. As we grow up, our hiding becomes far more sophisticated, but we keep the desire to conceal our shame.

One way we try to hide is by overcompensating for our areas of sin or weakness. If I have a weak arm, my other arm will develop greater strength to compensate. If I struggle with pride, I will develop the appearance of humility to compensate.

I have often found that when people begin to identify their signature sin, others are surprised by the name they choose. An intimate friend or family member might know my true self because they see me at my worst. More casual acquaintances have been fooled by the image I present to the world. They believe in the persona I portray.

Someone who is self-centered might develop the ability to appear very interested in others. Someone who is fearful might cover it with bravado. A dependent person might appear self-sufficient. The skills we develop to compensate for our signature sins may even lead us into our chosen career and life paths. Many of the students that I teach in the mental health field come from chaotic and dysfunctional families. They learned to skate above the chaos and put on an image that their lives are under control. Then they choose a profession where they make use of the skill of teaching others to be in control in spite of inner chaos.

One measure of maturity and mental health is *congruence*. It is the distance between the true self known by those close to us and the false self we present to the world. The public face is constructed to prompt others' approval. The private self is the face that we fear would be rejected. A less congruent person presents one face to the world and an entirely different face in private. A more congruent person has reconciled the two selves and does not present himself or herself in a significantly different way in public and at home.

Playing the part of an imposter requires practice. While we are busy hiding our private selves, the parts of us that are mean or fearful or stingy or self-absorbed, we develop great acting skills. Even though the reason for developing the skills is wrong, the skills themselves are real and effective.

Fortunately we have a God who loves to redeem the effects of sin. After their unhealthy purpose is removed, the skills remain. God does not waste anything. Even the skills we develop to hide our sin can be redeemed for God's purposes in our lives.

Now that we have explored the nature of our sins and the importance of combating our sins, let us turn our attention to the roots of our sins. We will move from the universal reality that everyone sins to the particular formulas which create individually unique patterns of sin. Why do you face some temptations and not others? Why does my pride look different from the next person's pride? Why can some people conquer their gluttony while others cannot? Many factors influence the unique patterns of our signature sins, for example, family, culture, gender and race. In the next chapter we will explore spiritual temperaments and how they influence our individual patterns of sin.

6

TAMING YOUR WAYWARD HEART

- When the idea of signature sins was introduced, did a name for your signature sin come to mind? If so, have you ever shared it with anyone? Write it down in your journal and pay attention to how your understanding of it grows through later chapters.

- How well do you know yourself?

  Do you feel you have a very accurate (humble) view of yourself?

  How well do others know you?

  How many people know you well enough to identify your signature sins?

- What mask do you present to the world to cover your secret self?

  How surprised would others be to learn of your signature sin?

- What events, relationships or unmet needs do you need to mourn?

  Do you avoid examining certain time periods or relationships in your life because they are too painful? Prayerfully consider how God would have you begin to mourn these difficult parts of your life.

- Set aside a half day for a spiritual retreat. Go someplace that promotes quiet reflection, such as a chapel, park, garden or library. Take along things that will assist you and not distract you from reflection: perhaps a journal, a Bible, helpful spiritual books, worshipful music or your favorite tea. Use this time to reflect on the idea of signature sins. As the following chapters explore the sources of these sins and their remedies, it will be helpful for you to have identified where your spiritual formation needs the most attention.

- Sit quietly for an extended period while you imagine sitting in the presence of Jesus. Ask Jesus to reveal to you how God sees you. Journal about those things you imagine him saying and about your reactions.

5

Temperament and Sin

ANY TIME HUMAN BEINGS ATTEMPT TO distill our experience of
God down to something manageable, we are doomed to fail. It took
two sexes to incarnate the image of God. It took two testaments, the
Old Testament of the law and the New Testament of grace, to contain
God's Word for us. It took four Gospels to communicate the message of
Christ's life through the different eyes and personalities of four writers.
God is one and yet exists in holy trinity. Jesus declared himself Lord
of every family, tribe, race and nation, of Jews and of Gentiles. Is it any
wonder that God's image-bearers come in every color, shape, size and
temperament imaginable?

God does not merely tolerate diversity in human life. God delights
in it. Paul described the church as a body, united yet consisting of
separate and unique parts (I Cor 12:12-26). The Holy Spirit gives
believers distinct spiritual gifts, all of which are needed in the church
(I Cor 12:1-11, 27-31). The relationship of Christ and the church
is like that of husband and wife joined in marriage to become one
flesh (Eph 5:22-33). As the body of Christ we are called not to put
up with each other but to delight in each other, not to tolerate each
other's differences but to cultivate a profound, undeniable need for
each other.

Each person's experience of the world is unique. No two people are exactly alike, even if they are born with similar temperaments. No two family members are even born into exactly the same family. Each child encounters a different combination of family members who are at different stages of their own development.

As a clinical psychologist I enjoy the opportunity to explore the fascinating puzzle that makes up a human being. No matter how much someone might look and sound like a certain category of people, I am always amazed to find the ways people fail to fit my pigeonholes. I work with many people who are trying to come to terms with the fact that they don't fit into the identity boxes provided for them. Every relationship is in a way a crosscultural encounter.

At the same time, I am always amazed at how much I have in common with every human being I meet. Several years ago I traveled to rural India. I talked with people who would seem to have little or nothing in common with me. Yet as we connected, our common humanity quickly outweighed all our differences.

As a Christian I believe that our universal humanness reflects the *imago Dei*, the image of God. This is why the incarnate Son of God could experience pain and temptation in a way that was universally human. "For we do not have a high priest who is unable to sympathize with our weaknesses, but we have one who has been tempted in every way, just as we are—yet was without sin" (Heb 4:15). At the same time I believe that our individuality also reflects God's image. Every member is needed for the body of Christ to be complete.

OUR INNER TERRAIN

Just as there are both universal and uniquely individual facets of every human being, there are universal and uniquely individual patterns to human sin. Every person may doubt that God is good, but my personal suspicions about the *ways* God may fail me will show themselves in the areas of my greatest vulnerability. While human strengths are universal, our vulnerabilities distinguish who we are. Like flaws in a diamond, they reveal our individual pain.

A life, like a landscape, has natural contours. Roads are carved where the route is easiest, not where it is most direct. Highways and country roads wind around for long forgotten reasons. The old obstacles are gone, but the road remains. Our patterns of thinking and behavior have similar meandering contours for long-forgotten reasons.

I grew up in a rural white community and in a conservative evangelical church. When I sit down with someone from a similar background, we immediately have stories to tell each other. We share similar ways of thinking, values and assumptions about the world. Other reasons for the terrain of our characters are not so obvious. Early relationship experiences have a large impact on the people we become.

Many people in psychotherapy experience the fear of expressing negative emotions such as anger or dissatisfaction in their relationships. Their pattern of avoiding honestly negative feelings causes them repetitive problems. Their relationships reach a certain point and can go no deeper. It is a common theme but it shows up with infinite variations. No two people have exactly the same reasons for experiencing this fear.

One young man sat down for his first psychotherapy appointment and tearfully described his father's suicide when he was an adolescent. Before the suicide his father and mother had divorced, and his father slipped into deeper and deeper depression. My patient wrote his father a letter expressing his anger and frustration at his father's increasing emotional distance. Soon after the son wrote this honest and courageous letter, his father hanged himself. Ever since, without realizing the reason, the son had avoided all conflict and expressions of anger. Instead he allowed anger to slowly poison his trust and intimacy from within. He had concluded that if he expressed negative emotions, the ones he loved would be devastated and would abandon him.

Another person came to therapy with a similar fear of expressing negative emotions. Her father was a seemingly charming person who was prone to fits of rage in the privacy of his home. This woman had to keep her hatred of her father secret or he would beat her. Though she was no longer under his control, she still avoided all expressions of her own anger. She feared that anger would grow into rage and that she would become like the man she hated most.

If you met both these people, you would say that they had similar personalities. They were both intelligent and charming. They had channeled their underlying anger into a quick, acerbic wit. Their relationships had a repetitive pattern of starting out well and quickly disintegrating at a certain point of intimacy. They complained that life had become numb and meaningless. I could tell many other stories of people whose patterns of living and relating look alike on the surface but who arrived there by different paths.

THE FOUR HUMORS

Despite individual differences, human thought and behavior fall into identifiable patterns. Traditionally these patterns have been called *temperaments* or *personalities.* They have generated many theories about their origin. I believe that we begin life not as blank slates but with a genetic predisposition of temperament that provides a framework around which we build a personality. Some studies suggest that we can begin to predict an unborn child's temperament by noting its activity in the womb.

Few aspects of psychology generate more fascination than personality theory. People take formal or informal tests to tell them which category their temperament falls into. Some people choose whether or not to marry a partner based on the compatibility of their personality profiles. People who believe in astrology explain themselves by the stars and constellations of their birth. Some cultures believe that the year of one's birth or a totem character associated with one's birth determines temperament. Most theories of temperament combine nature and nurture—biology and upbringing.

More than two thousand years ago Hippocrates, the father of medicine, popularized the idea that our temperament was based in our bodies. Bodily fluids called *humors* were thought to influence mood and behavior. Supposedly these fluids were generated by the body but could be influenced by foods, seasons, environment or other factors. We can see this idea's intuitive usefulness in the fact that the ancient names of the humors have become part of our everyday language. A person could be described as *sanguine* (cheerful, manic), *choleric* (angry, irritable), *melancholic* (depressive) or *phlegmatic* (calm).

The ancient personality types influenced Jung in his understanding of human archetypes. Jung understood temperaments according to where an individual falls along certain styles of approaching the world, such as introversion versus extroversion, sensing versus intuiting, thinking versus feeling and judging versus perceiving. The popular Myers-Briggs Type Indicator, one of the most widely used temperament scales, uses the same categories to determine its sixteen personality types.

My father and I had many discussions about temperament, although we didn't know we were discussing temperament. My matter-of-fact father often expressed puzzled amazement at the ways people behaved. As a budding psychologist, I intuitively understood even then that people would sometimes act in ways which made no logical sense from the outside.

A person's internal world—temperament, biology, experience, emotion and so forth—can outweigh all external influences. Anyone who has had life interrupted by a severe bout of depression can understand how an otherwise stable and sensible person could resort to suicide in order to escape from intense hopelessness. In the same way, alcoholism, infidelity, violence and other apparently unreasonable behavior have rational explanations.

The psychological profession is built on an assumption that understanding human thought, moods and behavior can promote change toward greater health and happiness. Through psychological means a person can be helped to change destructive actions, a child can be helped to learn in the way that fits the child's personality, a couple can be helped to transform unhealthy patterns of relating and a person can be guided to the career that makes the best use of the person's gifts.

Understanding temperament is also helpful in dealing with spiritual differences. Our style of relating to God is consistent with our style of relating to others. Our personalities influence our preferences in church and worship. It follows that an understanding of our temperament could be helpful in searching out the patterns of our sin.

Since our patterns of sin follow from our needs, hurts and hungers, one might expect that those with similar temperaments might struggle with similar sins. In fact, this is quite true. Different religious traditions and practices have always attracted people whose temperament fits them.

One helpful review of temperament and its effect on our spiritual lives uses four spiritual temperament categories: *Ignatian* (SJ), *Franciscan* (SP), *Augustinian* (NF) and *Thomistic* (NT). I will briefly summarize these temperaments, although no summary can capture their nuances or the Myers-Briggs typologies on which they are based. For a more complete description please refer to the original documents listed in the notes.

IGNATIAN TEMPERAMENT (SJ)

The Ignatian temperament is characterized by an emphasis on trusting concrete senses over intuition and trusting judgment over perception. Ignatius of Loyola, for whom this type is named, was a Spanish soldier and nobleman who was injured in battle. Over many months of recovery he experienced spiritual visions and developed the *Spiritual Exercises*, a series of ascetical disciplines and contemplative exercises that became influential in the formation of the Jesuit religious order. Ignatius was a loyal and chivalrous soldier for Christ.

Hippocrates' *melancholic* humor corresponds to the Ignatian temperament. People of Ignatian temperament prefer order and solid facts. They are practical and predictable and do not hunger for spontaneous or emotional forms of spirituality. This does not mean they are unemotional; they are quite passionate about what they believe. They prefer stability and tradition and rely on what is tried and true rather than on the latest fad.

Those of the Ignatian temperament are the backbone of the church. While others hunger for spontaneity and change, the Ignatian temperament maintains the church through passing fads and seasons. These guardians of the church will stand up for the truth and will faithfully work behind the scenes. If they see a problem, they want to fix it. If they see an enemy, they want to conquer it.

Ignatians' corresponding sins tend to be rigidity and idolatry. When tradition is valued over truth, spirituality can be drained of life. Ignatians' preference for the tangible and the stable can be stifling to other temperaments. Some Ignatians may one day realize that their faith has become a system of do's and don'ts rather than a vital relationship with God.

If, as Oswald Chambers argued, the root of sin lies in the suspicion that God is not good, the root of sin for the Ignatian temperament is distrust of God's grace and unpredictability. The Ignatian temperament is troubled by the God who pays the same wages to the worker who came at the end of the day and the worker who came at the beginning of the day (Mt 20:1-16). Jonah showed the same mistrust of when he refused to go administer God's grace to the Ninevites. The Ignatian temperament has difficulty trusting a God who is too easily swayed, who breaks his own rules and who works outside of the established order.

The signature sin of the Ignatian temperament is to doubt God's goodness, in that his ultimate goal of bringing the greatest number of people in line with his will seems thwarted by his grace.

The antidote to the signature sin of the Ignatian temperament will likely be some form of *surrender.*

Ignatius was a soldier. Surrender could never come naturally to him. His infirmities required him to surrender to the bed. He had to leave the war in Spain and enter into a spiritual war. His *Spiritual Exercises,* though satisfying his soldierlike need for discipline, also satisfy the spirit's need of surrender to God's transforming touch.

Those who hunger overly much for control, tradition and order will need to seek the antidote of surrender. Ignatius's *Spiritual Exercises* can be a helpful guide in this process. Ignatius taught his followers to read the Scriptures, especially the Gospels, in a very active way, imagining themselves as observers in the story. One might picture oneself at the event recorded in Mark's and Luke's Gospels when Jesus healed the paralyzed man whose friends lowered him through a hole in the roof. During the exercise one would imagine being a member of the crowd who observed the event. When fully immersed in the scene, one could imagine what Jesus might say and do. Then one might imagine talking to Jesus. What would you say to each other? How would it feel to talk with Jesus?

Ignatians' spiritual strength is their stability and strength in the faith. From the Franciscans (whom we discuss next) Ignatians need to learn greater openness to change and new experiences. From the Augustinian and the Thomistic temperaments Ignatians need to learn to trust the intuitive quest for what is true over insistence on what has always been.

FRANCISCAN TEMPERAMENT (SP)

The Franciscan temperament, Hippocrates' *sanguine* type, is characterized by a preference for the senses over intuition. In this way it resembles the Ignatian temperament. Unlike the Ignatian, however, the Franciscan prefers perceiving to judging. St. Francis of Assisi, for whom this temperament is named, saw his relationship with God as a passionate romance. He called himself a spouse of the Holy Spirit. He hungered for experiences of God's presence. Like St. Francis, such individuals will listen to God's call and abandon everything for the sake of that call.

The Franciscan lives in the moment. While the Ignatian distrusts perceptions and prefers hard-and-fast rules which don't require interpretation in the moment, the Franciscan fears that the vitality of the moment will be lost. Someone with this spiritual temperament loves spontaneous worship and hungers for the moving of the Holy Spirit. This temperament trusts experience more than tradition and trusts feelings more than doctrines. Traditions become stifling for Franciscans because rigid structures do not leave room for God to do a new thing.

The signature sin of the Franciscan temperament is being too easily swayed by passions and experiences. Franciscans hunger for sensual experiences—sights, sounds, smells, tastes, emotions—and they trust what those experiences seem to convey. Following after each new passion, they may too readily abandon old ways and be misled. In preferring perception over established order, Franciscans may abandon the stable structures that allowed for the creation of the sensual experiences in the first place. In welcoming the new they may marginalize those who feel most comfortable with the old. Those of this temperament will also hunger for action over contemplation. St. Francis cultivated a life of contemplative prayer, but he is most known for his actions, especially toward social justice. Franciscans prefer service over prayer. When prayer is pursued it is passionate, discursive prayer, filled with images and words.

The root of sin for the Franciscan temperament stems from the suspicion that God cannot be good if he seems far away. Franciscans hunger for passionate worship; they fear times of spiritual dryness. Their empathy for others makes it difficult for them to trust a God who condemns some to die and who chooses some to be his people while rejecting others. Franciscans welcome the God of love and grace, but they are suspicious of the God of wrath and judgment. They have trouble with a God who disciplines or does not come as experientially near as they would like.

Those of the Franciscan temperament have difficulty tolerating and appreciating times of God's quiet. Even if they practice silence and solitude as St. Francis often did, they will be filled with internal words and images. They might even tend toward sensual gluttony, hungering for a different spiritual experience every time. While they desire spiritual experiences, they may have strong preferences for certain kinds of experiences. Such preferences promote religious individualism, since experience is inevitably private.

The antidote for the signature sin of Franciscan temperament comes in the form of discipline. Since Franciscans are wary of being boxed in, they miss out on the structure boxes provide. The fear of the Franciscan temperament is largely a fear of sameness. Like all sins, it has a streak of pride. The same experience every day, especially if it is the same experience everyone else receives, starts to feel flat.

For the Franciscan temperament, submitting to routine and rituals is an antidote for the hunger after newness. Franciscans benefit from the practice of silent, listening prayer that seeks to still the heart and sit silently in Jesus' presence. Through consistent spiritual disciplines, especially seeking after external and internal stillness, Franciscans can learn to appreciate the steadfast and unchanging nature of God. Their spiritual wells can be dug deeper so they are less disquieted by spiritual dry seasons. They may even develop respect and appreciation for their stable Ignatian partners who normally vex them! From the Augustinian and Thomistic temperaments, Franciscans can learn to evaluate the truth and trustworthiness of what their senses tell them.

Augustinian Temperament (NF)

The Augustinian temperament is characterized by reliance on intuition over concrete fact and reliance on feelings over cognition. Where Ignatians look to tradition and Franciscans look to experiences, Augustinians trust their intuition. They value the past, but they look for the lessons the past teaches for the present, rather than assume that past traditions must be maintained. They value their own and others' experiences but understand intuitively the limitations of logic and the concrete senses.

Like St. Francis, Augustine of Hippo was a passionate man. His early life was largely governed by sensual passions which he later eschewed. His primary contribution to the church came from his passion for the life of the mind. His writings influenced the division between the Roman and the Eastern churches, led to the condemnation of the most virulent theological heresies of the day and provided the foundation for the Protestant Reformation. Augustine came to care deeply about character and integrity. He was an ancient psychologist in that he studied the inner workings of the heart and the disordered loves that lead toward sin and away from God.

Augustinians—*choleric* in Hippocrates' typology—seek meaning in the mystery of God's revelation. This temperament loves symbol and metaphor and paradox. They are more disappointed when the truth turns out to be simple than when it is too complex to grasp. Augustinians love the world of ideas and also love to share the world of ideas with others. They thrive on discussion and friendly repartee.

The Augustinian temperament is one of vision, dreams and adventures. A person of this temperament loves to promote change and creativity. Decisions are based on values and principles than on rules or tradition. The Augustinian hungers for silence and solitude to search inwardly for meaning.

The signature sin of the Augustinian temperament occurs when its strengths are taken to an extreme. Individuals of this temperament can use their intuitive sensitivity to manipulate others. Since those of this temperament rely on intuition, they can sin by reasoning that the old rules are too limiting and don't apply in this particular case. St. Augustine himself displayed the sins of this temperament more in his early life than in his later maturity.

Augustinians can elevate their own counsel over the counsel of others past and present and move toward moral relativism. They can take inordinate pride in their abilities to see layers of meaning. Augustinians can live so fully in a world of future idealism that they become detached from the people around them. They are optimistic but never satisfied, always hungering for new areas of personal spiritual growth.

Augustinians' suspicion of God's goodness stems from their abstract ideals and from their reliance on their own intuition over the authority of others. An Augustinian might speak eloquently of the God who comes to us in Jesus and gives us the Holy Spirit to be our comforter, but the lofty ideals of those statements never satisfy the hunger to feel God's warm embrace. The person of Augustinian temperament may envy those who receive powerful experiences of the Spirit's presence and may be tempted to artificially create such experiences. At the same time, the person of this temperament will not have the Franciscan's drive for passionate experience and may feel equal amounts of desire and fear for such experiences.

Those with the Augustinian temperament need greater attachment. They need the sensual world around them to bring them back to reality. They need to focus on others to pull them out of their own internal world. From the Thomists, whom we will consider next, Augustinians need to learn how to think through the truth or falsehood of what their intuition tells them.

The antidote for the sins of the Augustinian temperament is *humility* in the root meaning of the word *humus*, which means "ground." The Augustinian needs to be more grounded, less grandiose and more down-to-earth. The entrepreneurial spirit of the Augustinian must be balanced with the practical focus of the Ignatian or the here-and-now focus of the Franciscan or the right-and-wrong focus of the Thomist. Shared worship experiences are more helpful than contemplative forms of prayer in stretching the Augustinian. Praying in groups will help the person of this temperament move beyond the abstract world and into the practical realities of others' needs.

Thomistic Temperament (NT)

The Thomistic temperament is last in our list named for Thomas Aquinas, the great scholar of the church. Thomas Aquinas was a brilliant thinker who left a tremendous legacy in his written works and in the example of his life and work. Several universities and colleges are named after him. Many philosophers and theologians have been influenced by his thinking.

The Thomistic temperament (*phlegmatic* in classic terminology), like the Augustinian, trusts intuition over concrete experience. Unlike the Augustinian, however, the Thomist prefers thinking to feeling. Where Augustinians love to dream and envision new possibilities, Thomists want to live in the world of thought and intellect. They seek to have power over their world through logic and order, unclouded by emotions. They want to understand and explain everything and prefer to avoid all claims of mystery or paradox. When they acknowledge paradox, it is more as an intellectual reality than an experienced one.

Those of the Thomistic temperament are the thoughtful skeptics, the scholars, the teachers, the theologians and the scientists. Even in faith they seek order and sense, sometimes forgetting that faith cannot be reached through reason. Those who engage in logical debates on apologetics are usually of the Thomistic temperament. Thomists enjoy structure more than process and love to have clear, measurable goals to pursue.

The signature sin of the Thomist is intellectual snobbery. Thomists are tempted to feel contempt for others who are not so logical and disciplined in thinking. They may be divisive against those who believe differently.

Where the Franciscan will believe what he or she feels or experiences, the Thomist will believe what is concluded by reason or measurement. Preference for logic and order sometimes leads the Thomist to avoid the messy world of human relationships. Unlike the Ignatian who quickly fights to defend their truth, Thomists will often avoid relational conflict. They prefer to lecture rather than discuss. They are straightforward and honest and are genuinely confused when their directness wounds others. Thomists are often excellent teachers and may therefore become pastors, but they are not generally gifted in empathetic skills. The Thomist may be confused about how to care for the emotional needs of a congregation.

When the Thomistic temperament doubts the goodness of God, it is over God's apparent failure to keep his world and his followers in a more orderly state. For the Thomist right thinking and belief are almost always more important than intuitive experience, especially if experience seems to differ from established doctrine. The Thomist temperament seeks to use objective authority such as Scripture to answer every question of meaning and will often be quite literalistic in doing so. This temperament tends to be suspicious of God's goodness when any paradoxes of Scripture come to light.

Once while we were teaching a workshop on contemplative prayer, my wife and I encountered a man who insisted that silent prayer is dangerous. He believed that one should always be praying words or at least quoting Scripture because silence leaves room for improper thoughts and evil desires. His comments illustrate the extreme form of Thomistic temperament. Any experiences that don't fit exactly into the rigid structure of right thinking and belief are guilty until proven innocent. The strength of this temperament, its strong defense of orthodox belief, leads to the rise of authority figures who are entrusted with guarding the portals of truth.

The antidote for the sins of the Thomistic temperament requires the Thomist to acknowledge that the mysterious, messy world of paradox, emotions and relationships has value and truth that they cannot grasp. They must back off from their belief in the absolute sufficiency of the mind. Thomists must accept by faith that some truths cannot be measured and some paradoxes cannot be resolved. The Thomist must acknowledge that a life lived exclusively in the world of logic and right doctrine is ultimately unsatisfying without balance from the world of beauty and emotion. They need to embrace other aspects of worship besides the reading of Scripture and the sermon.

When I began attending an Episcopal church after growing up in a conservative evangelical tradition, many aspects of the liturgy powerfully moved me. The symbolic aspects of the liturgy and the church year spoke deeply to my soul. The Thomistic aspects of my upbringing left me hungry for a Christian spirituality that went beyond the mind. I wanted more than glorified lectures. I was also powerfully moved by healing prayer services and the doctrine of the real presence of Christ through the Eucharist.

My experience exemplifies the antidote for the signature sins of the Thomistic temperament. The soul needs more than proper theology. The Augustinian love of symbols and liturgies that capture depths beyond reason will help the Thomist, as will contemplative practices that speak as "deep unto deep." The Ignatian value of tradition will help a Thomist understand the importance of continuity with the saints of ages past, not only with those who agree with our brand of theology. The Franciscan can teach the Thomist a love of experiencing God in the here-and-now and in nature, in the heart as well as in the head.

AN ANCIENT ASSESSMENT

Another popular means for assessing spiritual temperament is the *Ennea-gram*. Its origins are unclear, but in the past century it has been popularized especially in Catholic circles. It is more of an oral tradition than a system or scale from scholarly writings.

Each of the Enneagram's nine personality types is associated with its own characteristic need and sin. The nine descriptive categories of temperament have an advantage over modern personality tests: they have stood the test of time. Contemporary personality tests line up with modern Western views of the self, while the Enneagram apparently comes from the ancient Eastern church.

Any discussion of the Enneagram is complicated by the fact that practitioners of astrology, Gnostic believers and New Age spiritualists have used it for purposes beyond the identification of temperaments. For this reason it is critiqued by Christian opponents. Others argue that Christians can use the wisdom of the Enneagram to help understand spiritual and psychological temperaments apart from non-Christian traditions.

Since the author of the Enneagram is unknown and it is not under copyright, it can be adapted to any specific use. Those who use it today often choose their own titles for each of the nine points.

Many have systemized the Enneagram into personality questionnaires that can be objectively scored and interpreted. When it is turned into a multiple choice quiz, we not only begin to lose its rich oral tradition, we also lose the traditional belief that one cannot identify one's own Enneagram type.

In the ancient spiritual traditions, people who were serious about their spiritual formation submitted themselves to the care of a spiritual mentor. Trying to examine one's own soul would be like performing a do-it-yourself appendectomy.

We must approach with caution the task of naming our own temperament and signature sin. Self-examination is an important part of the process of spiritual formation, but we cannot fully trust our own evaluation of ourselves. Our signature sins come about because of distortions

in how we see God, ourselves and the world. We are internally motivated
to avoid painful truths, especially about ourselves. We must check our
ideas against the perspective of another who knows us well.

With that caveat, here are brief summaries of the nine Enneagram
types. Over the years they have received various titles. I have used several
common titles for each.

Type 1: Perfectionist, Reformer, Critic, Judge, Crusader

This personality type is characterized by a focus on goodness and integrity and a need for perfection. In moderation this quality leads to disciplined moral living. At an unhealthy extreme the person of this type
develops a judgmental spirit. Their greatest fear is to be flawed. Suspicion
of God's goodness alternates between fear that God will see their imperfection and judge or abandon them, and frustration that God does not see
and judge the imperfection of others. Type 1's corresponding sin is *anger*.
Their anger alternates between self-loathing over their own imperfections
and righteous indignation at the imperfections of the rest of the world.

Type 2: Giver, Helper, Caretaker, Nurturer, Adviser, Planner

This personality type is characterized by loving care for and generosity
toward others. While other people value this person's generous spirit,
the immature person of this type can be something of a martyr. They
fear they will be loved only to the extent that they sacrifice themselves
for others. Their suspicion toward God is that God will withdraw his
love from them if they are anything but loving and "nice." Since direct
anger or aggression might lead to rejection, if they stray from their nice
persona it will be toward passive-aggressiveness. Ironically the classic sin
of this type is *pride*. They make themselves indispensable through their
selflessness and sacrificial nature. This type needs greater courage to
pursue their own wants and dreams rather than continually sacrificing
themselves for others.

Type 3: Performer, Achiever, Motivator, Producer, Magician

This personality type values success in the eyes of others. They are motivated to achieve and to be effective. Failure and obscurity are their greatest fears. They may be master showmen, charming everyone they meet. People of this type will be tempted to use their persuasive gifts to deceive others. Inwardly they often feel like imposters. They believe others admire them for their charm rather than for who they truly are. This type suspects that God will expose them as imposters and subsequently reject them. The sin of this type is *deceit*. They want to be judged on their outward accomplishments rather than their inner selves, and so they seek to hide their true selves and present only a polished successful façade.

Type 4: Romantic, Individualist, Artist, Dramatist, Mystic, Elitist, Afflicted Person

This personality type seeks uniqueness. Their greatest fear is to be plain and common. They can be depressed by the thought that they might turn out to be just like everyone else. Their creativity, idealism and expressiveness are wonderful gifts, but they are limited by moodiness and self-doubt. Their suspicion of God's goodness shows itself in the fear that God will not love them in a unique and special way. It follows that their sin is *envy*. While jealousy is the wish to possess and hold on to good things, *envy* is the wish to have what others have and to be the only one who has them. This personality type can learn to take great pleasure in their passion and giftedness; however, their desire for their own special relationship with God hampers their ability to nurture the faith of others. They need to foster a love of community, an acceptance of the ordinary and a servant's heart that is willing to be last and to let the last be first.

Type 5: Observer, Thinker, Investigator, Sage

This type of personality wants to be the one who knows everything. On the healthy side they are wise and understanding. On the unhealthy side they can be stingy, reclusive know-it-alls. They want to be valued for their knowledge, but they fear responsibility and the intrusion of others into their private world. They suspect that God will expect too much of them, especially in relation to others. They hunger for closeness to God and others, but fear what it will cost them. Their corresponding sin is *avarice*, hoarding resources and knowledge for oneself against the fear that others will exploit them.

Type 6: Skeptic, Trooper, Loyalist, Devil's Advocate, Defender, Guardian, Team Player
Those of this personality type long for a cause or a person that will give them stability by being worthy of their loyalty. They become anxious if anything makes them question the stability of what they stand for. They are slow to accept change and have experienced the unacceptable pain of questioning authority either personally or vicariously. They want to avoid standing out as different and being separated from the group in which they feel protected. While their strength is loyalty, their weakness is paranoia or cowardice. Their suspicion toward God is that he is an abusive or fickle master unworthy of loyalty. Their corresponding sin is *fear*. This fear is generalized rather than specific, but it becomes powerfully focused if any threat is made to their loyalties.

Type 7: Enthusiast, Generalist, Epicure, Adventurer, Materialist, Entertainer, Optimist
This type of personality is the class clown, the eternal Peter Pan. They seek fun and excitement, and they fear anything that will bring them down from their happiness. They bring a sense of spontaneity and playfulness to those around them; at their worst, however, they come across as aggressively cheerful and even escapist. They suspect that God will require them to give up their pleasures and face pain and difficulty. Those with this personality often struggle with the sin of *gluttony*. If pleasure is good, then more pleasure will be even better. They mistake quantity for quality and depth of pleasure.

Type 8: Leader, Boss, Protector, Challenger, Solver, Competitor
The personality of this type seeks to hold onto and wield power. They fear anything that could leave them vulnerable to being hurt or manipulated by others. Mature individuals of this personality are strong, confident leaders. In the immature state they can be vengeful power-hungry bullies. Their suspicion of God arises from his call to weakness and vulnerability. Like the serpent in the Garden, they suspect that a God who wants something all to himself must be holding out on us. The corresponding sin of this personality type is *lust*, not necessarily sexual lust but the lust for power and for all that life has to offer. They project their own lust for power onto others and cannot believe that others do not want to steal power away from them.

Type 9: Peacemaker, Mediator, Preservationist, Naturalist, Accommodator, Abdicator
The final personality type of the Enneagram seeks always to keep the peace. At their healthiest they are unpretentious and easygoing. At their worst they are passive conciliators who would rather go the route of appeasement than come down on one side or the other. Their suspicion of God is that he will call them to take an unpopular stand. Their corresponding sin is *sloth*, spiritual laziness. They accept the way things are, whether in the world or in themselves, without taking on the difficult and risky work of making anything better.

ONE HUNDRED PIANOS

Some people resist any discussion of the relationship between temperament and sin. They believe that we should be able to change our thoughts and feelings at will. It is true that most of us have experienced change in certain aspects of ourselves. Some of our patterns of thought, emotion and behavior reflect our circumstances; if we change our circumstances we can change some aspects of our inner life. If change was impossible there would be no point in writing a book like this one.

Nevertheless there are limits to how much we can change ourselves. Whether we call it temperament, personality or character, much of what makes up our essential self stays remarkably stable over time. We may be discouraged when we consider the biblical call to be changed into the likeness of Christ. I believe that God does not expect me to become someone that I am not, but rather to become the person he had in mind when he created me. Somehow, through the miracle of Christ's atonement, the Father sees me as his child. As I follow after Jesus, I grow to be the person God desires me to be.

In Proverbs the sage tells us how we should raise our children. "Start children off on the way they should go, / and even when they are old they will not turn from it" (Prov 22:6 TNIV). Every parent who has more than one child knows that "the way" is not the same for each child. I am always hesitant to teach classes or workshops on parenting because it is difficult to give principles that apply to every child and every parent. Some children cower at the slightest criticism; others require a much sterner approach. Some children have a natural desire to please others; some naturally put their own desires first. Parenting requires patience, attentiveness and prayer to find the right way for each child.

A similar principle applies to the way God parents us. He must approach each of us in the way that is right for us. We are all different, yet we are all called to be conformed to the same image of Christ.

A. W. Tozer was a wise and gifted pastor who knew the difficult struggle between private spirituality and universal truth. He wrote, "Someone may fear that we are magnifying private religion out of all proportion, that the 'us' of the New Testament is being displaced by a selfish 'I.' Has it ever occurred to you that one hundred pianos all tuned to the same fork are automatically tuned to each other?" What a wonderful image. One person might be a battered upright and another person might be a magnificent grand, but if they are tuned to the same master note, they will play in harmony.

The paradox of universality and individuality finds resolution in Christ. Our common tuning fork creates a church out of a bunch of misfits. Christ creates one body out of disconnected parts. In the chapters to follow we will explore the many factors, both universal and individual, that make up a human soul. We will then explore what can be done to help each soul find and follow the way that is right for that soul.

🐚

TAMING YOUR WAYWARD HEART

- Start to write your spiritual autobiography. You will continue it in later chapters. Tell the story of your first encounters with God even if you didn't recognize them at the time. In your earliest memories, how did you experience God's presence?

  Did others encourage your experience of God or did they try to change it?

- Which of the temperament categories seems to fit you best? Note them in your journal. For each one, list the ways God delights in your temperament and then list the ways your temperament hinders your relationship with God.

- Do you ever try to suppress your spiritual temperament to satisfy others?

  How would your worship and experience of God change if you were freed to act in a way more consistent with your temperament?

- Do you ever hinder others from expressing their spiritual temperaments?

  What are you afraid would happen if temperaments you don't like were given more freedom of expression?

- Which of the other spiritual temperaments do you most admire?

  Which do you most avoid?

  What does each one offer that you need in order to grow spiritually?

- What "type" of person do you want to be as you grow older? Is it realistic to expect yourself to become that person, or would it require unreasonable change?

6

Culture, Ethnicity and Sin

DESPITE GROWING UP ON A FARM, I am not a gardener and have no particular skills or interest in yard care. Consequently our family's yard sometimes gets into an untidy state. When I get around to cleaning up the back corners of the yard, I often find weeds that have grown unbelievably fast and tall. They are still easy to kill if they have not gone to seed.

I have been especially vigilant since I found a vine with poisonous berries in our yard. No matter how hard I work to find it and pull it up, it comes back the next year. Its roots are especially hard to eradicate since they travel underground and spring up in multiple places. Now the vine has wound its way into a patch of bushes, and the leaves of vine and bush are almost indistinguishable.

In my war with the poisonous vine I cannot afford to skip a season. The vine threatens to choke out the healthy plants and, worse, to offer its beautiful poisonous berries to unsuspecting children and animals.

Like the weeds in my yard, sin does not appear in our lives overnight unless its seeds sprout and are allowed to grow. New sins have shallow roots. We can deal with them if we do not try to hide them but admit that they need to be pulled up. If we don't root them out, they will flourish to become annoying and even dangerous.

Other sins have been sinking their roots down for years and sometimes for generations. They require constant diligence. If we do not regularly address them, they grow insidiously into every corner of our lives.

Some sin-seeds travel on the wind and easily take root if not attended to. Who is not capable of occasional petty jealousy or a lustful glance? Such sins are fickle, universal and easily uprooted. It is the sins that have been allowed to stay and grow that cause the most problems.

In our yard the worst weed problem is near the compost pile. There, both weeds and desirable plants find much nourishment. The most fertile places in our lives are the most tempting places for sins to grow. We are prone to hide infestations of sin in those most prized places. Think of the pastor or famous Christian author who condemns adultery, then is discovered in an adulterous relationship. The areas of our lives which are most in the public spotlight may suffer the most careless spiritual neglect.

When the Cameras Leave

I heard the story of someone who was spotlighted on one of those reality TV redecorating shows. The person's new home looked wonderful for a few days, long enough for the camera crews to get their images. Within days after the show was over, pillows came apart, moldings fell off and fixtures broke or had to be rewired. The renovators had done their work hastily and superficially. The cameras did not expose the underlying deficiencies.

Our spiritual lives, like that unfortunate person's house, need more than superficial makeovers. Even the most mature believer must continually look beneath the surface to find places where deep-rooted sins are peeking through the surface, ready to begin their destructive growth. This side of heaven I don't believe that any person can afford to be complacent about deeply rooted sins. Once superficial sins have been eliminated, it is time to begin searching for the telltale signs of roots awaiting their chance to spring forth again.

Some Christians have taken Jesus' words against pride and self-righteousness to mean that we should always feel worthless and unworthy of God's love. Such "worm theology" has left many people with a bitter taste in their mouths that they associate with the Christian church. Growing up in a fundamentalist Christian culture, I grew weary of the depressingly pessimistic worldview of many of my spiritual role models. It seemed that almost every sermon was about some sin that must be combated in ourselves or in our culture.

One extreme does not correct another. The Pharisee who sobs and sheds crocodile tears over his worthlessness is no more acceptable than the Pharisee who sings his own praises. Many of us learned at an early age that confessing the small sins leads to praise and admiration from others, as long as we keep the big ones to ourselves. It also leaves others assuming that if those are the worst sins we have to confess, we must have our sins under much tighter management than they do.

Like many who grew disillusioned with spiritual negativity, I fled in the opposite direction. For many years of my spiritual development I wanted nothing to do with depressing sermons about sin.

In recent years, however, I have grown weary of the opposite problem. In many churches we never hear sermons on sin and personal responsibility. Just as a believer in an overly moralistic church might starve for a sense of joy in God's love and grace, a believer in an overly accommodating church might starve for help in seeking after righteousness. Believers who are assured they are "good enough" receive no support in the process of looking beneath the surface of their spiritual lives.

Jesus does not call us to narcissistic humility any more than he calls us to narcissistic self-praise. What he longs for is that we would give up narcissism altogether. When I turn my eyes away from the obsessive comparison of myself with everyone else, I become free to love the Lord with all my heart, soul, mind and strength and to love my neighbor as myself. That type of love, Jesus declared, sums up all of the law. The goal is to lose self-centeredness altogether, not in a martyr-like way but in the wonderfully freeing way of the soul that has found its rest in God. To be freed of sin by the grace of God leads to the desire to help free others.

It is important to find balance in the search for sin. I do not need to examine every square inch of my yard for every kind of weed. I know which weeds I am likely to find and where they usually grow. Likewise I do not need to be always examining every detail of my life for something sinister. A beautiful well-kept garden is meant to be enjoyed. Those whose temperament leads them to be overly harsh on themselves should use this book to spend less effort on the search for imperfections and more effort where it really matters.

However, those whose temperament leads them to gloss over their sin should acknowledge the importance of a disciplined search-and-destroy mission. A garden that looks good only from a distance, or at only one angle at one time of day, is not authentically beautiful.

WATER FOR THE FISH

I enjoy teaching graduate students from many cultures around the world. From them I learn a great deal about my own culture seen through their eyes. For example, I have come to see that my culture is intensely individualistic, a quality which students from non-Western cultures especially notice.

From our culture we learn what to value and what to hold in contempt, what to hide and what to flaunt. The impact of culture is like the air we breathe or the water in which a fish swims. It is difficult to see until we are placed in an entirely different environment or until someone from a different environment helps us see it.

Just as families pass down traditions, cultures feed on the roots of their own history. From its democratic beginnings our culture fought for the rights of individuals over the whims of all-powerful royalty. The emphasis on the individual has had both positive and negative consequences. Newcomers to our culture praise its opportunities for each person to overcome limitations and achieve dreams not possible in other contexts. These same newcomers note our loneliness and disconnection from community.

Every human is a culture-bound being. Our patterns of sin also have a cultural context. Like individuals, cultures have signature sins. Cultures can even sin corporately. In the Old Testament, God sometimes condemned entire cities based on their collective sin. More recently, cultures that participated in the slave trade have suffered the generational consequences of their sin. Wars bring to light the best and worst in a culture in the mixture of motives for going to war.

People from an individualistic culture might tend toward sins of individualism such as self-centeredness and pride. People from a collectivist culture might fall into their society's sinful patterns of escaping from personal responsibility by going with the flow.

Some cultures believe in an idealistic, objective, universal form of fairness that should be accessible to all. Those from such cultures will hang onto the myth of such an ideal and ignore evidence to the contrary. Other cultures operate under a fatalistic assumption that justice is subjective and that fairness is only a myth. People in such cultures assume that those in power make the rules and naturally give preference to their own group.

THIRD-CULTURE PEOPLE

In the contemporary world some young people grow up shifting from one culture to another without having firm roots in any one place. Because of employment or mission work, their parents raise them in international settings but bring them up on stories of, and visits to, their "home" country. These "third-culture kids" have a culture of their own, neither the culture where they were raised nor the culture of their parents' roots. They feel somewhat rootless, but they are more able to rise above regional, religious or ethnic loyalties than those who know only one culture. They find their closest cultural home when they get together with other third-culture kids.

Christians are meant to be a third-culture people. The Bible speaks of those who were "longing for a better country—a heavenly one. Therefore God is not ashamed to be called their God, for he has prepared a city for them" (Heb 11:16). We are created for a heavenly homeland. We must resist the temptation to settle down in this temporary spot. We are meant to keep our eyes on the horizon where our country of true citizenship lies.

I have enjoyed two different forms of traveling in foreign countries. On some trips I travel with a group of American tourists. A tourist's encounter with the otherness of a culture is neatly and comfortably packaged. At the end of the day we all retreat to the familiar confines of a bus or a hotel full of fellow expatriates.

When I travel off the beaten tourist path, I have a quite different experience. There I see my fellow Americans and by extension myself through the eyes of foreigners. What I see is not always flattering but it is always enlightening.

We cannot confront the sinfulness we have inherited from our own culture without finding some way to step outside our own culture. Even then we must open our ears, eyes and hearts and be willing to see ourselves from a new and perhaps unsettling perspective.

It is frightening to introduce the subject of race and ethnicity. Few topics are more loaded with potential for anger and hurt feelings. As a white male I am especially aware of the risks of offering my opinions on race. I know that more avenues of voicing my opinion are available to me than to others. However I do believe that one's race influences one's patterns of sin.

Recently I took part in an activity in which racially diverse small groups were given cards with questions for the group to discuss. On each card was a question from one of several categories such as "Things Euro Americans might like to ask a person of color" or "Things a person of color might like to ask a Euro American."

One card was directed at the Euro Americans in the group. It asked if we are aware of the greater privileges that we have because of the color of our skin. It was a perceptive question. A signature sin of being white is remaining oblivious to the power, privilege and opportunities our race brings us.

I don't have to think about what it means to be a white male. I can choose to think about it and pat myself on the back for being noble and selfless. Or I can choose to pretend that it is an issue only if people of color make it an issue. In my culture a person of color—and in a different way a white woman—does not have the option of ignoring what it means to be a white male.

Early in my career as a psychologist I found out that women and people of color already knew how to see the world through my eyes. They had a better understanding of my world than I had of theirs. They told me it was because they have to live in the white male world every day. While I didn't want to believe this, one fact made it inescapable. They could describe my experience of my world without my telling them much about it. It has been a slow process, but through loving, patient relationships with women and people of color I am learning what the world looks like through their eyes.

RACIAL BENEFITS

Through much of human history you could be born, grow old and die without ever confronting a person who looked, spoke and thought differently from yourself. Such provincialism is hardly conceivable in the twenty-first century. Today the world is divided into (1) those who have the power to demand that others come over to their definition of reality and (2) those who do not. The nationalities and skin colors of the two groups vary depending on where you are in the world. The sin within the arrangement stays the same.

Those in the position of racial power are often entangled in the sin of pride. They may not participate in overt racism, but they enjoy the benefits that power has brought to their race and they never call their privilege into question. Some commit sins of cruelty and hatred which they have been taught are the privilege of their race. Others avoid outward manifestations of racism but commit the more subtle sin of sloth in their indifference and unwillingness to ask the hard questions and listen to the answers.

Those in the position of lessened power have their racial signature sins as well. I don't feel qualified to say much about them, but fallen human nature would dictate that they exist. For some, righteous anger turns unrighteous. For others, a unique kind of sloth takes hold, and like their privileged neighbors they become numb to the realities of injustice.

Even among Christians who take sin seriously, the sin of the racial divide is often the last sin to be addressed. Racial reconciliation is messy and frightening. Racial signature sins are not easily rooted out. Obvious sins of behavioral racism may be eliminated, such as racist jokes and discriminatory policies, while subtle racism remains.

Once I was asked if I had any African American colleagues at work. I did have one at the time, yet I answered no. I quickly realized my mistake and corrected myself. Later I told my colleague about the incident. Naively I reported that it was probably a good thing that I didn't think of her as black but simply as my colleague. She smiled patiently and explained that she appreciated the sentiment but, no, in fact it was not a good thing for me to stay consciously unaware that she lives in a world different from my own. As I remember our conversation I am embarrassed, but I am also thankful for her patience and the patience of others who have helped me open my eyes.

I live and work in an affluent Republican white suburb. I have
lived here for two decades. Although I confess to being rather flexible in my interpretation of the speed limit, I have never been pulled
over by a police officer. I remember the deep sadness and the sensation of now-I'm-starting-to-get-it when one of my African American students casually mentioned that he had been pulled over again
on the way to work, the umpteenth time that year, and how he
consciously sits up straight at the wheel and obsessively obeys the
speed limit.

One day I was walking across campus with an African American
student. I had recruited that student from her urban home and felt some
guilt about bringing her to an environment where I knew she would feel
out of place. I asked her to look around and describe what she saw as
if I were blind and she was revealing the world through her eyes. I was
humbled and moved at how different our environment looked and felt
to her than it did to me. Now when I walk by the same spot on campus
I often remember that moment of clarity.

OUT OF MY OWN MOUTH

From my childhood I remember another moment of more shocking
revelation. I grew up in a small Montana town and never "got out"
much. For years I was in the habit of saying that I never met an African American until I went to college. One day, well into adulthood, I
realized in a flash that my statement was not true. In my tiny school
there had been a black boy my own age. He must not have lived there
long because I remember only one interaction with him. We were in
the first or second grade. He was arguing with my best friend. I ran
to my friend's defense and, though I was normally a timid and passive
child, I angrily shouted "Black stinks!" My memory of the shock on
the faces of the boy and my friend is secondary to my memory of my
shock that those words had come out of my mouth. The boy ran away

crying and my friend confronted me about saying such a thing, but I was too dizzy, panicked and confused to even hear him.

Until I remembered that incident I had always asserted, like lots of well-meaning if naive people, that I was not a racist. I didn't tell racist jokes, I was friendly and kind to people of color and I abhorred the racism I saw on TV. I remained blissfully unaware that racism resided in me at deep levels I couldn't easily access. I grew up in a good Christian home. No one explicitly taught me to be racist, but somehow I soaked it up.

My race has committed racist sins and I have indirectly benefited from them. I can no longer deny that truth because for one moment generational sin reared its ugly head and used my tongue. I have never been the recipient of a racial slur, but somewhere there is an African American man my age who has likely received many, and one of them was from me. I wish I could ask him for forgiveness.

SEEING THE WATER

Most of us like to associate with people who make us feel comfortable: people who look, sound and think like ourselves. To uncover the deep roots of prejudice requires the eyes of another. People of another race must teach me those things they wish I knew. In order for that to happen, people of other races must be willing to bridge the gap and tell me the truth.

I will not realize how being a Euro American has influenced my signature sins until I first *know* that I am a Euro American. That sounds obvious, but it is not so easy to achieve. To know myself as a person of a certain culture, I have to try to look at myself objectively. Somehow I have to be able to see the water I swim in. Objectivity will come only if I pursue experiences and relationships that foster my awareness of my own culture.

As we examine our hearts for the effect of race on our signature sins, it is good to look to community. By *community* I mean diverse community. In subsequent chapters we will address ways to open ourselves to others who are not like ourselves. But first, let us examine the impact of gender and family on the nature of our signature sins.

TAMING YOUR WAYWARD HEART

- Add to your spiritual autobiography. What is your culture and how has it influenced your relationship with God?

   What is your race and how has it influenced your relationship with God?

- Spend time in your prayer life asking God to reveal to you how your culture might contribute to your sin patterns.

- Is Jesus of your race? If you are white, the correct answer is "no"; yet many of us were implicitly or explicitly taught that Jesus was white. How does race affect your relationship with Jesus?

- What do you value in your culture's faith traditions, and what could you do without?

- How do your culture and/or race affect your struggle with sin?

   Have they pushed you toward certain kinds of sin?

   Have they sheltered you from others?

- Look around your church, home, school, workplace and other places where you spend time. Do you notice variety in culture, ethnicity and gender?

   Have you asked others about their experiences of God and the world? Ask God to open your eyes to see him through the eyes of others.

- Immerse yourself in an experience outside of your comfort zone. It may mean attending a house of worship of a faith other than your own, attending a family event with a friend from a culture different from your own, or traveling to a different neighborhood, city, state or country. Do everything possible to stay away from tourist activities. Try to experience the way of life of the locals. How flexible and open are you to connecting with and understanding the experiences of others? Journal about your experience.

7

Gender, Family and Sin

GENDER IS INTIMATELY INVOLVED IN ANY discussion of sin because we cannot understand sin apart from the place and the principal characters of its origin. When we think of the Fall of humanity we lump Adam's and Eve's sins into one event. In reality they faced different temptations and sinned in different ways. As a consequence, the signature sins of men and women tend to differ from each other.

One of the most articulate discussions of gender and sin that I have read is by Mary Stewart Van Leeuwen. She notes that God commanded both Eve and Adam to have dominion over the earth. Each disobeyed the command in a unique way.

The serpent tempted Eve to overstep the boundaries that God had placed around dominion. Eve wanted to gain even more knowledge rather than depend on God to differentiate good from evil. Adam's temptation was quite different. Eve had already eaten the forbidden fruit. Adam's choice would seem to be to join Eve's disobedience or to remain separated from her.

Eve idolized dominion while Adam idolized social unity. Van Leeuwen points out that each gender suffers from a *contra coup*, a mirror image injury associated with their sin. Eve overstepped dominion; as a result, women place undue emphasis on maintaining relational unity at all costs, even avoiding responsible dominion in family and society. Adam experienced eviction from the Garden as a result of desiring social relatedness; as a result, men place undue emphasis on dominion to the exclusion of relationships.

Some Christians argue that God's intended order is for men to follow their natural inclinations to take dominion and for women to tend to family and relationships. Others counter that men's and women's natural tendencies are not what God intended but rather are distortions of the Fall.

MUTUAL SUBMISSION

When my wife and I were engaged to be married, we had many discussions about gender roles and biblical views of manhood and womanhood. I had been taught that the man must be in charge in the relationship, otherwise the marriage will descend into chaos when the two disagree about the course their life should take. In this view it is a sin to have an egalitarian marriage. I thought then and still think that the argument makes little sense. If a husband and wife discern God's will differently, why should the man's discernment be trusted over the woman's? Why not assume that the man is equally likely to be distorting God's message?

I have heard the answer that Eve was more easily tempted than Adam and sinned first; therefore a woman's nature cannot be trusted for decision making. In my opinion it is more likely that men have a fallen tendency toward the sin of overstepping dominion and that women have a distorted desire to maintain harmony at all costs and go along with males' leadership.

In marital roles I am an egalitarian. I am convinced that mutual submission in marriage fits Christ's call more fully than does a traditional interpretation of male headship. I will be quick to say, however, that I have heard articulate arguments for a headship model that take a more sophisticated and nuanced approach than "the man is boss." In the Ephesians 5 discussion of husbands' and wives' roles, the husband is to love the wife as Christ loves the church. Some traditionalists articulate that such sacrificial love transcends gender stereotypes and values the woman's perspective in all things.

I used to have lively discussions about marital roles with a psychologist colleague who has since gone to be with the Lord. We settled on a compromise. I asked him what he thought about my wife and me having been committed to an egalitarian marriage for over fifteen years. He thought for a while and then said, "That's your prerogative. As the head of the relationship you can choose to base your marriage on that model."

GENDER IMPACT

Gender's impact on sin goes beyond marriage. The effects of the Fall on gender affect every person and all human relationships. Biology and environment—nature and nurture—define our experience of being male or female. If your experience of gender fits historical and cultural stereotypes, you likely struggle with the signature sins of detachment and dominance for men or enmeshment and conflict avoidance for women.

Gender is never neutral. We may enjoy the blessings that come with our gender or curse its restrictions, but no one can deny that gender plays an important role in our formation as human beings. It certainly wields strong influence on our patterns of sin.

I once worked with a couple who were both miserable in their marriage. The husband was artistic and warmly relational. The wife was a practical, no-nonsense hard worker. The husband hated his job and wished he could stay home to raise and homeschool their children. The wife hated childrearing and felt she could be much more productive in a career outside the home. When I suggested that they reverse their marital roles, they looked at me in horror and asked how I could suggest such an unbiblical idea. They assured me that their pastor and church would never support such an arrangement. This couple and their pastor believed that their sin was lack of conformity to the biblical model of a family. In their worldview there was no room to consider that God might have gifted them in ways different from traditional gender roles.

In our endeavor to name our signature sins, we should assess the ways in which gender has influenced our patterns of sinning. We should also explore ways that our attempts to fit fallen gender stereotypes have twisted our view of ourselves.

A man in my church once stated, "Of course God didn't intend women to lead. Look around and see how few women leaders there are." The argument was irrational. We cannot have it both ways. We can't argue that how things are reflects how they ought to be, then argue that sin has corrupted creation and the world needs to be redeemed.

Redeeming the effects of the Fall on gender means seeking what God truly intended when he created man and woman in his image, then separating God's original intention from its later distortions. What parts of our concept of femininity and masculinity authentically represent God's designs for woman and man? We must seek God's guidance to see gender as God intended it to be.

Gender and Anger

When I began to study the writings of the contemplatives, I noticed that with several shining exceptions there are few women among them. There are many desert fathers but few desert mothers. The literature was primarily written by monks for monks. Even the women whose wisdom has been collected wrote to other women who set their lives aside for complete devotion to God through a religious order. The Christian contemplatives were a select, disciplined and primarily male group. It is not surprising that their guidance for a holy life is infused with testosterone.

I make this point because I believe women's voices have too often been left out of historical conversations about sin. The omission especially shows up in the conversation about the sin of anger.

In the classic spiritual formation literature, admonitions about anger have a distinctly male tone. If you look at the world from a male perspective you would conclude that the sin of *anger* means *anger out of control*. Most people with anger problems whom I have known or worked with have been men. When I counsel women about anger, I find that for every woman whose anger is undercontrolled there are several women whose anger is overcontrolled. Female victims of violence are typically under the power of someone who has proved to them that their anger will only lead to more severe abuse. They cannot choose to voluntarily surrender their anger because they are not capable of tapping into any awareness of their anger.

The Lost Voice

Several years ago my friend and colleague Cynthia Neal Kimball and I surveyed college women about unwanted sexual experiences. The women wrote their stories anonymously. Although we read some accounts of date rape and sexual abuse, more than half of the stories were accounts that we came to call stories of the "lost voice." The women recounted being with men who did not overpower them in any literal way yet left them feeling violated. The men in the stories were often youth pastors or other figures who held powerful roles in the women's lives. These women wrote things such as "NO! was running through my mind but I just couldn't say it till afterwards" and "I couldn't say no to a guy even though I knew I should. I was not forced to do anything—I just didn't have the strength to say no." The women seldom blamed the men or spoke of themselves as victims. Instead they described feeling confused and ashamed that they could find themselves in such a situation and not know how to get out.

Many of the women connected their vulnerability to unwanted sexual experiences to what they had been taught about men's and women's roles. Some noted that they had been trained to defer to men and to doubt their own judgment. Messages they hear in church about being godly women often become internalized into passivity and a lost voice. I have found this in many Christian women. They feel they should never speak out against others, even in the face of injustice.

As noted earlier, Mary Stewart Van Leeuwen suggests that Eve's sin of overstepping dominion led to the signature sin of women avoiding responsible dominion. In general, she asserts, women emphasize relationships over appropriate power and authority. That was the pattern we found in the young women's stories in our study. They were afraid that if they said no, they would be rejected or abandoned by the men who held power over them.

ACTIVE SURRENDER

In light of such strong gender inequality, how do we discuss the signature sin of anger? When I think of developing a humble, gentle and submissive spirit, I think of Paul's exhortation to take on the attitude of Christ Jesus: "Who, being in very nature God, / did not consider equality with God something to be grasped, / but made himself nothing, / taking the very nature of a servant, / being made in human likeness. / And being found in appearance as a man, / he humbled himself / and became obedient to death— / even death on a cross" (Phil 2:6-8). The attitude of Christ is the spirit of submission and surrender which the desert fathers wanted to adopt for themselves and instill in those to whom they ministered.

When I read this Scripture passage, though, I am struck by all the active verbs. Jesus was a servant, a fairly passive role, yet all the verbs are active. Jesus *made* himself nothing and *took* the nature of a servant. He *humbled* himself and *became* obedient. Those are not things done *to* him but things he actively chose. One who knows he has a right to claim authority may actively relinquish it. But what if one hasn't yet learned that one may take authority?

As Van Leeuwen notes, the sin of men is to take inappropriate authority, even sacrificing relationships to do it. In this light the writings of the desert fathers make perfect sense. They were men teaching men how to submit to the contemplative life. If the signature sin of men is to overstep the bounds of dominion, then dealing with the sin of anger is of central importance. Anger is often triggered by obstacles to our pursuit of personal power.

Anger in women usually takes a different form. Women's anger will not be touched off by frustrated power but by wounded relationships. The teachings about avoiding the sin of anger can lead to guilt and confusion for women who already have difficulty believing they have the right to be angry.

Women must know that they have a right to authority before they can imitate Jesus and willingly give it up. Women must know that they can take responsible dominion before they can be expected to relinquish it. Women must know that it is right to feel anger in the face of injustice, especially injustice toward themselves, before they are asked to forgive.

Many women have more than enough access to their capacity for anger; many men suffer from the opposite extreme. The point is not that all women need to feel more anger and all men need to feel less. The point is to tailor the cure to the disease. Every person, female or male, should look to his or her own heart for the ways that anger leads to sin.

FAMILY PATTERNS

Our families have the greatest influence on our development, including the development of our patterns of sin. Some people even assert that family curses are passed down along generational lines. The belief comes from Old Testament passages which say that God "punishes the children and their children for the sins of the fathers to the third and fourth generation" (Ex 34:7). I will leave that discussion to biblical scholars. Whether or not families inherit spiritual curses, it is obvious that patterns of sin are passed down through families. Everyone sins; but just as culture, ethnicity and gender steer our patterns of sin in particular directions, so do our families.

In my work as a therapist, I am amazed at the intricate ways in which family patterns of sin haunt people, even without their knowledge. I have seen individuals have an extramarital affair, only to learn afterwards that a parent had an affair at the same age. Many parents lament that they replicate the unhealthy discipline habits of their own parents, despite all their promises to themselves that they would not repeat their parents' mistakes.

My family of origin is known for avoiding conflict. While this characteristic makes us easygoing and friendly, it also means that grudges sometimes fester under the surface without being resolved. Other families go to the opposite extreme and get addicted to conflict. They can't connect with each other except through fighting.

I clipped out a cartoon of a person sitting alone in a room full of empty chairs next to a sign that read "support group for people with perfectly healthy, well-adjusted families." Psychology graduate students often say their parents are afraid that the student will come home and point out all the pathologies of the parents and the rest of the family. Their fear has some basis because every family has its own areas of health and dysfunction. Unless the family is unusually abusive or otherwise unhealthy, however, most students come to realize that their own family's quirks and neuroses are no worse than those of their fellow students' families.

One measure of a family's health is its capacity for members to tell each other the truth. This sounds obvious, yet many families live under astonishing layers of lies. A person sincerely trying to grow spiritually may have to acknowledge family as one source of sin, only to meet resistance from others in the family. Fear of facing sin patterns robs families and individuals of the opportunity to confront and vanquish the sin. Reconciliation is not possible when only one party acknowledges that a wrong has been committed.

Children are very suggestible. Parents easily exploit children's vulnerability to having their perceptions altered by steering a child away from one interpretation of reality toward another. Guiding a child's thinking is harmless and even helpful if, for example, I steer my child away from wanting soda toward wanting milk for breakfast. It is insidious, however, if I steer my child away from seeing that I have sinned toward believing that he or she has sinned. A cruel, abusive mother lies to her son, telling him that the beatings are for his own good. A hostile, controlling father tells his daughter that her mother left because the daughter was such a bad girl.

Those who have been subtly and systematically lied to often have great difficulty sorting out the truth. Others find them easy to exploit. I sometimes ask patients to watch the classic 1944 movie *Gaslight.* Ingrid Bergman plays a woman who is slowly convinced by her psychopathic husband (played by Charles Boyer) that she is losing her mind. She comes to trust his perceptions over her own, even the obvious fact that the gaslight in her room has dimmed, suggesting that someone has turned on a light elsewhere in the house. When a detective following the husband notices the dimming lamp, the woman is flooded with relief to think that her perception of reality is trustworthy after all.

THE FAMILY TRAITOR

Families who want to present an image of perfection often demand that family members keep all family sins a secret. Secrecy shackles people in their search for wholeness. When they ask for greater honesty from their families, even when the affirmation that their sadness or anger over these patterns is legitimate, other family members deny the problem and refuse to discuss the issues. The one who wants to talk about the underlying truth is often branded a traitor.

A graduate student studying to become a psychologist told me of a holiday trip to see her family. She wanted to talk to them about some painful family patterns that she was struggling to deal with. Afterward she was confident that she had not been disrespectful or provocative, yet her family's vitriolic denial of the problems stunned her. Her family— well respected and admired in their church and community—refused to entertain any such discussion.

In some families the layers of deception run so deep that there are multiple versions of the "truth" and even siblings can't agree about what is true. I have consulted with two couples who found themselves dealing with children and/or grandchildren who accused the husband of sexual abuse. In both cases the children spoke quite convincingly of recovered memories of the abuse. The men maintained equally convincingly that it had never happened. Each of the men insisted that their accusers had False Memory Syndrome, a phenomenon in which memories are fabricated in the mind of a suggestible subject. In one case the evidence of abuse became so overwhelming that even the man's wife was convinced he was lying. In the other case it never was clear what was the lie and what was the truth.

I have worked with clients whose families essentially cast them out because they called attention to hidden patterns of family sin. When they expose the family's problems, the identifiers are brought to psychotherapy as the troublemaker of the family. Like the ancient practice of laying sin onto the scapegoat (Lev 16:6-10, 20-22), the family projects its pathology onto the one who refuses to act like everything is fine. These scapegoated individuals long for an honest acknowledgment that their anger at their family is justified. The longer the family withholds the acknowledgment, the longer the traitor's banishment continues. If the family can rally and honestly own the legitimacy of the criticism, the family's unity can be restored.

Whether or not the family acknowledges its patterns of sin, a person searching for paths of righteousness must face and name those generational sins in order to keep from passing them on to the next generation. Sara Groves has a wonderful song about this simple but profound concept. In her song "Generations" she sings:

Remind me of this with every decision
Generations will reap what I sow
I can pass on a curse or a blessing
To those I will never know

Speaking the painful truth is one of the greatest gifts one generation can give to the next. Sin denied breeds corruption from within. Sin confessed can be exorcised.

☉

TAMING YOUR WAYWARD HEART

- In your spiritual autobiography discuss the way in which your gender has affected your spiritual life. What parts of that effect do you value?

  What parts of it frustrate you?

  What do you feel the church taught you about your gender?

- *Women:* Is it difficult to relate to Jesus as a man?

  Does the use of male pronouns to refer to God affect your relationship with God?

- *Men:* How does the biblical metaphor of the church as the bride of Christ affect you?

Do cultural attitudes about gender make it difficult to embrace surrender and servanthood as Christlike virtues?

- Have you ever worshiped in a group made up only of your gender? Attend such a service if possible. How is the experience of worship different from mixed gender worship?

- In your spiritual autobiography discuss the role of your family tree, both immediate and extended, in your spiritual life. What spiritual legacy has been passed down to you?

  What parts of that legacy do you embrace?

  What parts do you seek to disown?

- Are there particular sins in your family which feel like a curse passed on from generation to generation? Request a meeting with your pastor, spiritual director, spiritual friend or fellowship group. Ask them to pray over you, particularly praying that the roots of your family sin will cease to have control over you. Journal about the experience and about the ways that becoming free from the hindrance of that sin will revitalize your spiritual growth.

- How many generations of your family have been godly? If your family is not currently committed to Christ, can you find a past generation that was? If your family is Christian, can you trace the roots to the first generation to turn toward Christ?

- In your journal, draw a family tree. Fill in sinful relational patterns that have existed through the generations of your family.

  What sinful patterns are you helping to maintain?

  What sinful patterns are you helping to end?

8

The Biology of Sin

WHERE IN THE BODY does the soul reside?

Many Christians have the misconception that at death the soul is released from its physical bondage and lives throughout eternity unencumbered by flesh. They disregard the biblical teaching of the resurrection of the body. Without realizing it they have adopted a type of modern gnosticism rooted in the suspicion that the body is bad and the spirit is good.

Christian orthodoxy teaches that human beings are created in God's image. The human body is part of what God pronounced good at creation. Our bodies are affected by the Fall, but in themselves they are not evil. After our fallen bodies die we will receive glorified bodies.

Jesus became incarnate in human flesh not to redeem the disembodied human soul but to redeem the total person including the body. When he returned to his followers in flesh and blood after the resurrection, Jesus showed what our own resurrection bodies will be like.

St. Francis of Assisi is said to have referred to his body as "brother ass," a vehicle for carrying his burdens and serving his spiritual needs. On his deathbed he reportedly apologized to his body for his overly ascetic practices. Like Francis, we often view our bodies as objects in which we temporarily ride, forgetting that we *are* our bodies and that our bodies are the temple of the Holy Spirit (1 Cor 6:19).

Thoroughgoing naturalists want to reduce humanity to the level of physical bodies. When they say that we *are* our bodies, they mean that when our bodies die we cease to exist. Even Sigmund Freud, the champion of the world of the unconscious mind, never challenged the physiological presuppositions of his professional training as a neurologist. He believed that all psychological experience could be reduced to neurological systems. Though neurology never advanced to the point of providing physiological explanations for psychological phenomena, Freud never abandoned his core beliefs. He remained a naturalist, denying the existence of the supernatural.

EMBODIED SOULS

The fact that all human experience can be reduced to biological processes, particularly in the brain, does not require us to accept philosophical naturalism. Christians believe that we are eternal beings. We are more than temporal flesh and blood.

We can be *supernatural dualists,* believing in eternal life free of sickness and death in a new heaven and new earth, while also being *mind-body monists,* believing that the soul is embodied and that the body will be resurrected. I do not claim to understand all the mysteries of death and resurrection. I believe in bodily resurrection, but it is a mystery how the essence of "me" will continue to exist between the biological death of my fallen body and my resurrection into a redeemed body.

We are holistic *souls,* not spirits or minds with separate bodies. I am my body as much as I am my mind or my spirit. Although I am convinced of this truth about myself, it is still disconcerting to realize that what I experience as my mind is ultimately the firing of neurons coordinated by three pounds of flesh within my skull.

Christians who want to grow spiritually must address the reality that sin is both spiritual and physical. Everything about our experience of ourselves and of the world ultimately comes through one final common pathway, the neurological system within the body.

Sometimes we speak romantically about going back to the Garden. We mean we want to recover a time of innocence. In a similar way we speak of wishing we could go back to our childhood. Few of us would truly want to be children again. What we mean is that as adults we wish we could feel, again, the freedom from responsibility and fear, the innocence, the optimism and the simplicity of childhood.

Adam and Eve in the Garden represent not the ideal but the infancy of what God intended for humanity. Heaven represents the culmination of God's plans. When I am honest with myself I don't long for Eden. Instead I long for eternity with God, where I will get to keep all I've learned and all that I've become. I will also gain the incorruptible sight of God's goodness and an unquestioning dependence on the sufficiency of his care for me. All of our longings which we try to satisfy through sin are variations on our one longing to be reunited with God in heaven.

Sarx and Sōma

Two Greek words in the New Testament are translated "flesh" or "body": *sarx* and *sōma*. Biblical scholars note that the words are often used interchangeably but have subtle differences. *Sarx* connotes a more crude reference to the body, akin to meat. *Sōma* has a more polite connotation and is generally used in reference to the goodness of the body.

Paul used *sarx*, the baser of the two words, when he referred to our fallen inclination to hunger for sensual pleasures more than we hunger for eternal things. Sensual desires themselves are not evil. What Paul condemns is an inappropriate hierarchy. Just as candy is a treat we can enjoy in moderation if we are also nourished by good food, the desires of the flesh are good and appropriate in their ordained place.

Emotions are tied to biology. Every emotional state has associated bodily responses. Whether they are stimulated first by outside experiences or by internal thoughts, every emotion takes place as a physiological change.

When a person sees an upsetting event or recalls an unpleasant experience, the brain stimulates the adrenal gland to secrete adrenaline. The heart beats faster, blood pressure increases, the pupils dilate and several other changes take place in the body. The person feels the physical changes and associates the physical sensations with the emotion of the experience.

A shot of adrenaline, also called epinephrine, will produce the same physical reaction. People with dangerous allergies may carry epinephrine to inject themselves if they encounter their allergen. If the same person receives a shot of epinephrine when not having an allergic reaction, the person will experience the physiological symptoms of being emotionally upset. A person with a tumor on the adrenal gland may experience random bouts of intense physiological arousal.

Here are three distinct events which can cause the same physiological state, what we call the fight-or-flight reaction. In the first case the arousal is caused by a real experience in the world, such as being in an accident. In the second case the reaction is induced by an injection of artificial adrenaline. In the third case the reaction is caused by an illness. All three cases result in a similar emotional experience.

Now imagine a well-meaning pastor or family member who assumes that a person's anxiety is evidence that the person does not have sufficient faith in God. If the person's body is reacting to the presence of excess adrenaline, it makes no sense to tell the person that the lack of ability to stop the reaction is sin. Similarly it makes no sense to say to people whose levels of serotonin are severely disrupted that they should be able to will away the symptoms of their depression.

I am not promoting some form of biological determinism where no one is held responsible for actions induced by emotional responses. Our response to biological forces which influence us should not be resignation but grace.

Like Job's friends, well-meaning Christians advise their depressed neighbor to pray and to remember God's love or even to examine his or her life for sin. While the advice is fine for the spiritual and cognitive aspects of depression, it leaves a gaping hole where the biological is concerned. A friend or neighbor may struggle against biological forces greater than yours. I have experienced severe depression. My experience enables me to have deep sympathy for someone who struggles to cling to the smallest bit of hope and finds it slipping away.

Healthy Mourning

As a psychologist I must always address the bio-psycho-socio-spiritual elements of a person who is struggling. When a person's brain has come to a state of severe depression, nothing improves quickly. The physiological state of the depressed brain takes time to heal.

I never rule out miracles, but in my experience God more often chooses the slow and natural means of healing psychological disorders. Depression and other psychological disorders usually have physiological components which do not respond quickly to any intervention. A person may be doing important psychological, social and spiritual work to bring change; the biological causes for the disorder, however, may not respond to these interventions. Sometimes the biological roots of psychological pain need to be treated with medication. Sometimes they respond to the introduction of new habits like exercise and improved sleep patterns or the abandonment of bad habits such as substance misuse or an unhealthy relationship. Some disorders such as schizophrenia and bipolar disorder may require a combination of all these interventions.

Some people have never looked within themselves to face the losses, abandonment, anger or other pain that life has dealt them. When they start to face their losses, they begin to feel the pain they have been avoiding. Their emotional pain becomes embodied in physiological symptoms. Sleep becomes disrupted. They feel restless. They experience anxiety attacks, increased blood pressure, aches and pains. They cannot concentrate or make decisions. They are plagued by obsessive thoughts or ideas they cannot turn off. Their appetite increases or decreases. They gain or lose weight.

There is nothing strange about their symptoms. Neither are the symptoms necessarily a sign of personal sin. They can be perfectly natural manifestations of healthy psychological growth—signs of mourning. People who are addicted to comfort cannot imagine how such pain could be normal and healthy.

Folks often come to a psychologist seeking to have their pain eliminated as quickly as possible. They visit their physician or a psychiatrist asking for a pill such as an antidepressant, hoping it will make the pain go away. When I suggest to them that the best way out of their pain is to move in toward the pain, they are shocked. Actually, more often the family and friends are shocked. People in pain often know intuitively that they have inner spiritual work to do, and they sense they have the inner strength to make meaning from their pain.

Far too often people are counseled out of the healthy stage of mourning. Friends or family want the person to "get over it" so the pain is ended and everyone's life can go back to normal. They tell the suffering person that lack of faith must be causing the depression or anxiety. Because of this stigma, people often hide their depression. Or they may complain of vague illness; physical symptoms are more socially acceptable than psychological ones. Depressed individuals will often confide that it was easier to explain to their spouse or parents that they are experiencing heart palpitations and lethargy than that they feel frightened and hopeless most of the time.

RIPE FOR MATURITY

Those in great emotional pain feel alone. They assume no one will understand. When a patient comes to me in deep psychological pain and with many physical symptoms of anxiety and depression, I typically respond that I am excited to see that they are so ripe for movement to their next stage of maturity. The person's sense of relief is palpable. Very often the most powerful intervention I can provide is also the simplest: to normalize their pain.

It is important to understand the biological component of being human before we can truly understand sin. What happens in our bodies and what happens in our minds are inextricably linked, but the way they are related is never simple.

One way to say it is that depression, anxiety, rage and other problematic emotions are always caused by sin; however, *the sin involved is not necessarily that of the individual.* Our bodies, designed by God in God's likeness, experience crippling fear, depression or rage because they inhabit a sinful world. My own sin may cause me to become depressed, but so may the ways that I am sinned against. To make it even more complicated, my depression may be caused by a combination of my own sin, the sins which have been committed against me and the general sin of a fallen world which gave me faulty genes.

Freud was one of the first psychologists to systematically face the link between psychological pain and physical symptoms. Many of his early patients had strange physiological symptoms which could not be explained by traditional medicine. This category of patients proved frustrating to Freud and other physicians of his day. Freud discovered that with the "talking cure" many of his patients' neurological symptoms disappeared. When varieties of causes for people's physical symptoms began to be explored, their neurological conditions improved. Much of modern psychotherapy has been built on this discovery.

Freud likened the emotional and neurological system to an arrangement of hydraulics. Wherever the flow of emotional energy is obstructed, there will be a build-up of pressure. If the pressure becomes intense enough, it causes discomfort and dysfunction.

I prefer the image of piling sticks and rocks across a stream. A pool develops behind the dam while the stream continues to bring the pressure of more water. People are afraid of what will happen if the dam breaks. They may be flooded with overwhelming pain, fear, anger or exhaustion. They need someone to stand with them as they pull a few rocks and twigs from the dam and allow it to collapse. The flood they feared is often remarkably small. In fact it usually takes less energy and time to bring resolution to their pain than the time and energy they invested over the years in avoiding the pain.

THE SPIRITUALITY OF ANTIDEPRESSANTS

My optimistic perspective on psychological pain has some exceptions. Some people have such enormous lakes of pain behind their dams that they would drown if it were all released at once. These people need years of slow and careful work to dissipate their hurt from a life of abuse, neglect or loss. Other people are crippled by more severe physiological symptoms of anxiety and depression than can be tackled by psychotherapy alone. They have genetic predispositions to mood disorders.

Disorders which affect the psyche are more integrally involved in our spirituality than are other medical conditions. If I have cancer, but have a sense of hope and trust that God will care for me, it is a much different struggle than if I am depressed and incapable of mustering any hope at all. This should make us all the more eager to treat dysfunctions in the brain that keep some people from feeling the full extent of God's love for them.

The biological and psychological sides of anxiety and depression always go together, but sometimes a particular person's combination of symptoms will lean more one way than the other. Some people are so crippled by the physical symptoms of depression that they cannot get out of bed to come to a therapy session. Others have such severe anxiety that they cannot leave the security of home. Or they are so immobilized by lethargy that they cannot concentrate enough to make use of counseling sessions.

A person who is rendered powerless by physiological symptoms of a severe mood disorder should not be expected to work through the disorder by psychological or spiritual means alone. In that case I ask the counselee to seek a consultation with a psychiatrist or other physician. I am dumbfounded when patients or their family members respond that they believe Christians should not take psychotropic medication. They expect to be able to resolve their illness with prayer alone.

One young woman, referred to me by her pastor, told a story that truly astounded me. After years of infertility, she had become pregnant but then experienced a miscarriage. Due to complications from the miscarriage she had to have a hysterectomy, which threw her into immediate menopause and ended her hopes for children. The surgery led to complications that required her to go under the knife, under general anesthesia, two more times. She was normally a cheerful and energetic young woman known for her positive outlook and willingness to help anyone in need. Now she was severely depressed, struggling to get out of bed in the morning. She felt lethargic and hopeless. She received no pleasure in anything. She even found it difficult to pray or attend church. Nevertheless she was praying diligently for healing, as were her husband and members of their church.

When I asked this woman why she had not gone to her physician to ask about antidepressants, she replied that she and her husband believed that her problem was a spiritual issue. If she prayed with enough faith, God would heal her. With encouragement and education about a Christian view of medications, this woman was able to receive help from a physician in the form of an antidepressant medication.

I have become convinced that Christians' resistance to the use of psychiatric medications is a contemporary form of the ancient heresy of the Gnostics. The Gnostic sects of the early Christian centuries denied the humanity of Christ. They believed in the superiority of spirit over flesh and could not accept that God would be incarnated in a physical human body. With special knowledge one could transcend the limitations of the flesh. In popular usage the term *gnostic* has come to be applied to any system which values spirit over body and supernatural over natural. Many Christians unknowingly affirm this ancient heresy when they speak of the soul being resurrected without the body.

Christians who resist psychotropic medications adopt gnosticism in the sense that they believe supernatural forms of healing are superior to biological forms of healing. They deny that we are embodied souls and instead believe that our spirits are separate from our bodies. It is one's spirit that is sick with depression, not one's body. Such dualism is not consistent with orthodox Christian teaching. The body is spiritual *and* the soul is physical. Both should be treated with equal reverence as God's creation, broken by the Fall, redeemed by Jesus' bodily death and resurrection. On those grounds, refusal to consider taking an antidepressant could be a sin.

Of course God can heal depression or any other illness by supernatural means; but for whatever reasons, God does not always choose to work miracles. In this fallen world we should be working to redeem the effects of the Fall. If we can do that by seeking a cure for cancer or developing better antibiotics, why is it less acceptable for Christians to use medicines that work to redeem the effects of the Fall on the human brain?

The most common forms of psychotropic medications prescribed today are a form of antidepressant and anti-anxiety (anxiolytic) drugs known as Selective Serotonin Reuptake Inhibitors (SSRIs). Without going into the biology of the action of these drugs on the brain (which is not my specialty) it is reasonable to say that they are relatively safe and effective. These medications free many from chronic and severely debilitating forms of depression and anxiety. In many cases the medications literally transform people's lives.

Having said that, I must admit there are problems with psychotropic medications, as we would expect in a fallen world. While they are not addictive in the sense of creating dependency, they are a tempting escape for those who do not want to do the difficult work of facing the pain and loss which caused their depression in the first place. Where depression and anxiety have become incapacitating, medication can free a person of enough symptoms that the person can face and tackle the wounds of the past. We should never use antidepressants as a magic escape to avoid the vital work of inner healing.

Anyone who has taken an antidepressant or an anxiolytic will attest that it isn't that simple anyway. These medications sometimes have troubling side effects. They never take away the events or the circumstances that led to our pain in the first place. Medications are not the complete answer, but neither is the attempt to survive debilitating depression on sheer guts alone.

A PATIENT LIKE JOB

It is still disconcerting to think that my spirituality—my experience of being an eternal soul who participates in God's plans for the universe—is mediated by my brain. I have studied this subject for years and still sometimes I don't want to believe that. It cannot be fair that some people are more biologically predisposed than others to feel happy and hopeful.

For years I worked with a man I called my Job patient. This man wrestled mightily with depression and anxiety all his life. A devout Christian believer, he struggled to be faithful in his prayers and in his trust of God. He was a loving husband and father and provided well for his family. He engaged in psychotherapy with perseverance and honesty in his attempts to uncover any psychological or spiritual sources for his pain. He remained open to any word from those around him of sin he needed to confess. In short he was the perfect patient, doing everything he could do to facilitate his own healing.

My Job patient also pursued all available medical means for help. Over the years, under the direction of his psychiatrist, he tried every one of the antidepressant categories that might have provided any alleviation of his symptoms. He did it all with no success.

Like Job's friends I sat with him. I could do little else. Over the years we exhausted every type of intervention I could think of. I often questioned whether I could be as faithful as he was under the same circumstances. We separated after several years when I ended my work at the practice where we met. I have to admit, though I'm ashamed to say it, a part of me was relieved to end our work. As I sat with this man I could understand the temptation to be like Job's wife, who gave up and encouraged Job to curse God and die. After our work together had ended, as if his plight was not enough, I heard that he contracted a severe and debilitating disease. I often think of him and wonder how he has fared. He taught me much more than I taught him.

How do we explain cases like this man's? I would vehemently disagree with anyone who claimed my patient did not have enough faith or did not pray fervently enough for healing. Was there some untried pill that could have ended his suffering? Was there some spiritual or medical intervention we didn't try? Of course I can't answer these questions. I have worked with other people like this man, people whose situations resisted all forms of healing and seemed utterly hopeless. I carry enough of their stories inside myself that I have little patience for trite answers about having enough faith or following the proper spiritual path to healing.

On the other hand I have seen enough instances of powerful spiritual and psychological healing to keep me from giving up on miracles. I have a great respect for those whom God has gifted to be healers.

I once attended a healing conference. It was excellent with a balanced and humble view of the power of prayer for healing. As part of the training, participants broke into groups to practice praying for people's healing. Sometimes nothing apparent happened. In other cases the prayers led to remarkable results.

Some of the people for whom we prayed had struggled for years with closely intertwined spiritual, physical and psychological illness. During the prayer sessions I found my mind wandering to the next day, next week or next year of the person's life. I knew what changes would be required after the healing. I knew that some aspects of the healing would need to continue for weeks or months. At that conference I realized more clearly than ever before that God gifts some people to administer miraculous immediate healing, and God gifts others in the art of slow, patient healing. The body of Christ needs healers of both types.

To those who pray for immediate healing and an end to their pain, either through supernatural or medical means, God sometimes answers no. In God's perfect plan there are reasons why long-term struggles are often best for the development of our souls. By itself, ending psychological pain is not an adequate goal. The most significant growth in human character typically comes through pain. Jesus did not promise that a life of following him would be free of pain. On the contrary, he charged us to take up our cross and follow him. We will not always know why God leaves us to struggle, just as Job did not know why God allowed him to suffer. At those times the best thing we can provide to each other is a reminder that God is good, even when we do not feel like it.

BIOLOGY AND RESPONSIBILITY

I can only briefly comment on the final point of this chapter: biology and responsibility. The topic itself is far too big to tackle thoroughly, and it is outside my specialty. Everyone who watches the news or reads the paper knows that our culture wrestles with the question of responsibility in light of biology.

Courts consult forensic psychologists to determine a defendant's mental capacity to understand his own behavior. Some are judged not guilty for reason of insanity. Some have even been defended with arguments about the influence of junk food on their mental state.

Among Christians, responsibility in light of biology is an inflammatory aspect of the debate over homosexuality. I believe that in all but the most exceptional cases, a predisposition to homosexual desire is instilled at an early age by biological and/or psychological factors. It is not fair to call such developmentally instilled desires a choice. Some push the argument further and insist that if one has no choice about being attracted to one's own sex, the person should not be denied the right to fulfill those urges.

Suicide is another issue which raises questions about responsibility in light of biology. The Roman Catholic Church has long taken a hard line against suicide. People who took their own lives were once denied Christian burial. Anyone who has experienced a major depressive episode knows the reality of the powerful and frightening urge to end the pain and escape this existence. How do we judge the responsibility of someone who takes his or her own life under the crushing weight and reduced capacity for reasoning that come with the biological illness of depression?

We could name many other controversial areas of responsibility and biology. Many people have a biological and/or psychological predisposition toward substance abuse and addiction. Others have tendencies toward physiological arousal that push them to fits of rage. Still others wake up in middle age and realize that forces beyond their control trapped them in a joyless and loveless marriage before they were mature enough to make such a crucial life decision. Every day most of us struggle with family legacies and biological temperaments which steer us toward certain kinds of sin. How do we measure responsibility in light of the countless external factors which act on our will and assault our freedom to choose?

I've painted myself into a corner because I have no satisfying answer to my own question. I certainly cannot escape it. I deal with this question every day in my role as a counselor and adviser to people who are trying to live their lives in the face of hostile forces.

The Intersection of Law and Grace

How can we be held responsible for what we did not choose? The question lies at the exact intersection of law and grace, where many of the bitterest theological battles are fought. Since this book is not about judging others' sin but rather is about judging one's own heart, I will not tackle the broader question of determining someone else's culpability. Instead I will focus on how we examine ourselves.

We are all tempted to blame our sin on someone or something other than ourselves. In the Garden Adam and Eve hid from God because they feared the consequences of their sin. When God confronted them, Adam blamed Eve, and Eve blamed the serpent. The serpent had already blamed God. When he was little, my son—definitely the child of a psychologist—once proclaimed, "It isn't my fault; my brain made me do it."

Since most sin is motivated by the suspicion that God is not good, we can point the finger of blame within ourselves, in our hearts where the suspicion lies, and outside ourselves, in the people and circumstances that feed our suspicion. Once we become aware of the influences over us, we are responsible to turn around and exercise control over them. If I have become sufficiently aware of outside influences on my free will to complain about them, I no longer have any excuse for blaming them.

Maturity means that I take increasing responsibility for myself and that I spend decreasing time and energy avoiding my responsibility. The spiritual disciplines handed down through the centuries will help us fight this battle within.

TAMING YOUR WAYWARD HEART

- In your spiritual autobiography, write about the relationship between your body and your spiritual life.

    Do you embrace and care for your body as the temple of the Holy Spirit?

    How has illness or other limitations of the body affected your spiritual life?

- How does your body uniquely struggle with sin?

    In what ways do the weaknesses, strengths and needs of your body lead to temptation?

- What do you believe about physical healing?

    When you are ill do you feel comfortable asking for healing prayer?

    Do you believe that God answers such prayers?

- In listening prayer, ask for guidance in how God might be calling you to care for your body differently than you do now.

- How has suffering—your own or others'—influenced your spiritual life?

9

Spiritual Disciplines to
Tame the Wayward Heart

I OFTEN FILL OUT RECOMMENDATION LETTERS for students who
are applying for jobs. Twice over the years students have applied to a
particular mission agency which sends its own evaluation form to be
completed about the applicant. One of the questions on their form is
"Does this candidate have any tendencies toward asceticism?" I always
reply, "I hope so."

Although my response is a bit sarcastic, I understand what the
agency is looking for. Ministries are wise to watch out for unhealthy
self-denial in areas where people are known to push themselves to
harmful extremes.

Despite its dangers, asceticism has its appropriate place. We should
not use it as a synonym for self-abuse. Appropriate ascetic practices remind us of how easily we become addicted to comforts of the flesh.

I have been delighted to discover in adulthood the traditions of
the church year practiced in liturgical congregations. I am especially
moved by the practice of Lent, a time of spiritual preparation for the
feast of Easter. For me the simple ascetic practices of Lent are refresh-
ing and transforming.

In my nonliturgical background, Easter was a nice Sunday that usually caught me by surprise and was forgotten just as quickly. When I was introduced to Lent, I chose some simple ascetic practices to prepare my heart for the miracle of the resurrection. By fasting one day a week and giving up some luxuries or adding some spiritual disciplines, the six-week season of Lent became a welcome time of self-reflection. After a period of quietness and voluntary self-denial, especially during Holy Week, I experienced the joy of Easter as never before.

Every good thing can be spoiled. Asceticism has a bad name because some people take it to extremes. My pleasant discovery of Lent in adulthood is countered by stories of those who were forced to experience Lent as a time of sullenness and guilt-induction.

ORDERING THE APPETITES

The forty-day period of Lent (six-and-a-half weeks minus Sundays, which are always feast days) is patterned after Jesus' forty days in the desert following his baptism (Mt 4:1-11; Lk 4:1-13). During that time Jesus fasted and faced Satan's temptations. One of the temptations was to change stones into bread and end his fast. Jesus' reply, "Man does not live on bread alone," shows the importance of rightly ordering our appetites.

In other contexts Jesus affirmed the goodness of feasting and care for one's body. In the desert, however, Jesus modeled the importance of putting the desires of the body in their proper place. The needs of the spirit should not be neglected while we attend to the needs and desires of the body. Voluntary ascetic practices are meant to help us order our appetites.

Each year during Lent I pray about what practices the Holy Spirit might call me to for that season. During many Lenten seasons my wife and I have fasted together for one day each week. We are always surprised at how difficult it is. For this fast we do not eat between the evening meal of one day and the evening meal of the next. We are simply skipping two meals and snacks, yet we find ourselves scheduling the dinner which ends the fast earlier and earlier each week!

When I deny myself those meals and snacks, I am always surprised at how obsessed with food I become. My awareness means that asceticism is working. I am humbled at my childish feelings of anger and the rationalizations I contemplate for breaking my fast early.

THE GOD OF PLEASURE

Today we equate the sin of sloth with laziness. In the early church the term had more of a connotation of spiritual indolence. A monk who was overly attentive to the needs of his body was considered slothful. If he had a sniffle and chose to stay in bed rather than go to early morning prayers, he might be encouraged to consider his priorities.

In North American culture we are extremely attentive to the desires of the body. For many of us pleasure has become a god. Ascetic practices offer a helpful corrective to the worship of pleasure. Paul admonished us to rightly order our appetites. " 'Everything is permissible for me'—but not everything is beneficial. 'Everything is permissible for me'—but I will not be mastered by anything" (1 Cor 6:12).

Readers who have been wounded by harsh ascetic traditions will feel understandably resistant to my praise of asceticism. I have encountered many people who are unable to practice anything ascetic without taking it to an extreme. Where one person might fast for a day, they feel compelled to fast for a week. They neglect their own health while they attend to their spiritual responsibilities. Their self-inflicted martyrdom is not the same as healthy asceticism. After it causes temporary discomfort, ordering our loves should bring joy and peace. Ascetic practices are not ends in themselves. Their aim is to bring us nearer to God.

People who have overly self-critical temperaments or who have been abused by others' critical demands are often better served by disciplines of self-care than self-denial. During Lent I have often encouraged people to add something rather than take something away.

For example, if a mother attends to everyone in her household but herself, I would encourage her to arrange an evening out with friends every week while her husband feeds and bathes the children. I have encouraged some people to rise thirty minutes earlier every day, not to engage in discursive prayer or Bible study but to sit quietly on the porch with a cup of tea. I have encouraged many to take a retreat, a period of time in a quiet place away from all the daily routines and responsibilities.

MINIATURE DESERTS

The purpose of ascetic practices is to break us free from all our usual distractions. Ascetic practices are meant to create miniature deserts in our lives. Few of us can set apart forty days to go out into the wilderness for contemplation. I must admit that I find it difficult to remember to set aside even half an hour in my day to contemplate my life in relation to God. I have no excuse for avoiding those miniature deserts. I think I am a little afraid of what I will see if I go there.

Enemies of solitude and silence have proliferated during my lifetime. My laptop computer, phone and MP3 player all provide music I can listen to anywhere. My cell phone and email make me available to others at any time. I have heard people talking on their cell phones in toilet stalls and at urinals. Groups of kids walk by, each talking on a cell phone to someone else or each listening to his or her own music headphones.

My daily commute is now a time to catch up on phone calls. I get up early for a quiet time with God and feel like I am being sucked over to my computer to check my emails. Recently I took a call from a patient while I was sitting by a campfire in northern Wisconsin. Once I led a retreat and nearly took along some work to do during the meditative time. My perceptive wife reminded me that I might want to use the time for my own prayer and meditation!

I want to say clearly that I enjoy technology (just ask my family). Technology itself is not to blame for the neglect of silence and solitude. Technology cannot do anything harmful to us unless we allow it to do so. To paraphrase a popular saying, iPods don't distract people; people distract people. The difference today is that even the times that used to be silent and alone are now filled with sound and connection. We must expend extra effort to discipline ourselves to seek solitude.

I once asked my spiritual director to recommend what I should take along with me to read or study on an upcoming spiritual retreat. He paused for a long moment, looked puzzled and replied, "I don't think you should take anything." He told me that he had never given that advice before and wasn't sure why he had said it. I quickly assured him that he was in tune with the Holy Spirit. His words had struck me as correct—and frightening. I exhort others to seek silence and solitude, but it is no less difficult for me.

FEW SEEK SOLITUDE

My greatest wish for times of spiritual retreat is that God will show up. My greatest fear is the same, that God will show up. In the silence I may hear God's voice and I may be undone by what I hear. Frankly on most days I would rather listen to my iPod.

I know I'm not alone in my ambivalence about solitude. The retreat center that I have enjoyed for years is closing. For decades it has provided a quiet place for encountering God, but now there aren't enough people seeking spiritual retreat to pay the bills. Even contemporary Christians who are serious about deepening their relationship with God would rather do it at a weekend workshop full of lively teaching and praise music than alone in a room at an isolated retreat center.

Pascal studied the human tendency to forsake the pleasure of solitude, which he called the greatest source of happiness, for the lesser pleasure of noise and activity. He noted that people prefer the chase to the quarry. When we cease from chasing after things and stop to contemplate what we have, we find no comfort. He concluded "all the unhappiness of men arises from one single fact, that they cannot stay quietly in their own chamber."

When we allow ourselves to be constantly diverted from silence and solitude, we become lost, exactly as I would become lost if I drove without pulling my eyes away from billboards or without stopping to look at a map. The word *contemplate* comes from a root that means to *see* or *observe*. It has the same root as *temple* or sacred space. When we set aside time for quiet solitude, we create a space to contemplate and to observe the sacred.

My musical tastes are eclectic. In my computer MP3 player I have a folder titled "Songs of Longing." In that folder I put songs which communicate a message of longing or evoke a sense of longing in my heart. I began to collect songs of longing after a colleague introduced a meeting by having us close our eyes and contemplate eternity with God while he played "Beyond the Sky" by Fernando Ortega. For a few minutes each of us experienced a taste of longing for the day when we will be united with our Father in heaven.

In my folder I have songs from many genres: rock, folk, jazz, classical, gospel. Some are well known; others are obscure songs which I tracked down after I heard them on the radio or at a concert. What all the songs have in common is that the artist somehow captured a sense of longing for things to be complete, whole and unbroken.

I have tried to make longing into a spiritual discipline for myself. I find it both pleasant and uncomfortable. I don't think I am unusual in my constant drive to cultivate contentment with how things are in my life. While there is nothing wrong with being contented, contentment has become an addiction when I construct illusions that everything is fine and nothing needs to change. Contentment becomes sloth when I take my eyes off the horizon where my hopes lie and keep them focused only on the present.

Longing breaks through the illusion that everything is fine the way it is. I am encouraged in the practice of longing by my favorite passage of Scripture, Hebrews 11:13-16. The writer has been describing Abraham and other giants of the faith. Then the writer goes on to say:

> All these people were still living by faith when they died. They did not receive the things promised; they only saw them and welcomed them from a distance. And they admitted that they were aliens and strangers on earth. People who say such things show that they are looking for a country of their own. If they had been thinking of the country they had left, they would have had opportunity to return. Instead, they were longing for a better country—a heavenly one. Therefore God is not ashamed to be called their God, for he has prepared a city for them. (Heb 11:13-16)

Every time I meditate on this passage, it disrupts my world. I am always surprised when other people aren't taken aback by it. When I read this passage I hear the writer challenging me to give up all illusions that I can have a home in this world. I am condemned to always be an alien and a stranger until I die or the Lord returns.

PERPETUAL DISCONTENT
God wants to be the God of those who are perpetually discontented. We aren't called to be cynical or negative or distrustful, but God does call us to be discontented.

The idea of perpetual discontent flies in the face of everything that our culture tells us about happiness. It challenges the notion that happiness is even something worth pursuing. In some ways Hebrews 11 praises the saints of history for their discipline in staying unhappy. They could have settled in a comfortable place, but they did not settle; they kept going.

I am always ambivalent about preaching the message of perpetual discontent. It sounds uncomfortably close to the guilt-inducing sermons I heard as a child. It would be easy to get caught up in the negative implications of never settling in this world and forget the staggeringly positive implications of what it is we are waiting for. The patriarchs aren't praised for being unhappy; they are praised for remembering that their true happiness lies in heaven. They are praised for not making an idol out of this present world and its fleeting comforts. They are praised for keeping their loves in the proper order.

As we examine our hearts for sin, it is tempting to focus on the negative side of the search, eliminating sin, and lose sight of the positive purpose, to clear space where God can provide us with something better in its place. When I open my heart to longing, I have to look around and see that things are not how they were meant to be. I also open my heart to feel the excitement of knowing that someday my longings will not only be fulfilled, they will be surpassed.

Oases in the Wilderness

The exodus of the Israelites out of Egypt and into the Promised Land is the foundational story of the Old Testament. I have never been to the desert in which they wandered, but I grew up on the great American plains and I know a bit about wilderness. As part of her graduate study my wife studied the history of the old West. She told me of reading the journals of settlers who traveled across the plains in wagon trains. Most of them intended to make it all the way to the Pacific coast, but the journey was filled with hazards. Along the way people fell ill, family members died, animals died or winter came on earlier than expected.

Forts and settlements along the route provided respite for those who could not complete the journey west in one trip. The pioneers' journals tell of many people who, after spending the winter in one of the settlements or after recovering there from an illness, decided to stay and settle in that place rather than continue on to the end. Towns along the old wagon train routes are populated by descendants of people who meant to go all the way to the west coast and stopped short of their goal.

There is nothing wrong with travelers changing their plans, but the settlers who cut short their journeys show how attractive it is to settle for something short of our original goal. In the same way it is tempting to stop short on our journey of becoming conformed to the image of Christ. It is easy to settle for halfway there, plop down and say, "I've changed about as much as I want to change." The journey is arduous. Oases along the route begin to look like pretty comfortable places to build a permanent home.

I'm sure the Israelites were tempted to stop at some of the oases where God let them rest. If not for the pillar of cloud and fire moving on, they probably would have stopped and stayed. I assume that they had no choice but to follow the source of their protection and provision while they were in the desert.

The patriarchs who are praised in Hebrews 11 had a choice. They could have gone back to the country from which they had come. We also have a choice; we can settle for second best and content ourselves with where we are right now. God's desire for us is that we keep our eyes on the horizon and remember that we are strangers and aliens in this land, while we are preparing ourselves for the home that has been promised.

Not Future Only

How do we prepare ourselves? Jesus did not call us to sit and wait. Dallas Willard in his compelling book *The Divine Conspiracy: Rediscovering Our Hidden Life in God* demonstrates that the kingdom of heaven is truly at hand. We are not waiting for something that is for the future only. We can enter that kingdom now and become the kind of people who give evidence of Jesus' presence here and now. Heaven will be a beginning of sorts, but it will also be an extension of the transformation that begins in this world. We are preparing our souls now for the work God has for us in heaven.

Too many believers live as though once they are saved there is nothing left to the Christian life except saving others. Too many Christians focus on salvation and neglect sanctification. They ignore the reality that coming to saving knowledge of Christ is only the beginning. We have before us the exciting pilgrimage of pursuing Christlikeness ourselves, not just telling others about it.

Self-examination is part of the process of seeking Christlikeness. Self-examination is not a game of solving puzzles and keeping rules. It is a process of gradually submitting one's soul to God's transforming touch. I can't willingly release to God what I have not acknowledged to be part of me, and I cannot seek to look more like Christ until I know what Christ looks like. Once I have seen his face, I will want nothing more than to look less like my old, sinful, broken self and more like the soul that God intended me to be.

Sloth is not the default human condition. Jesus attracted crowds because he talked about what they were hungry to hear. He did not just tell them what to stop doing; he taught them how to live. He promised that there is a good way to live and that it is within reach.

Seeking to name and confess our signature sins is only half of the equation. If I confess my sin, I have removed an obstacle that keeps me from God. Now I need to step closer to him. If our signature sins are a poison to which we have become addicted, we need to take an antidote. If we want to complete the task of fighting sin in our lives, we must seek after righteousness.

Goodness does not automatically seep into our lives when the sin is removed. We must actively seek goodness. Just as we need to discover and name our signature sins, it is important to name the virtues which should take their place.

POISONED GIFTS

In an earlier chapter we discussed the importance of coming to know ourselves so well that we can name our signature sins. Each name we choose shows our familiarity with our own personal pattern of sin. The names will become even more important as we consistently seek forgiveness and help from the Holy Spirit in ridding sin from our lives. Naming is equally important when it comes to the antidote for each signature sin, that is, the virtue with which we seek to replace it.

Sin is not always directly opposed to the good. Often it is just a little bit off-center. Put another way, what is sin in one context might be good in another context. When Eve ate of the forbidden fruit she took initiative and dominion, something God had commanded Adam and Eve to exercise over creation. The sin was in the choice of fruit from that specific tree because God had withheld it from them. Adam's choice was also a sin, even though he maintained relatedness and a common experience with his wife. In most other contexts that would have been a good rather than a sinful choice.

Signature sins are often twisted virtues. I have confessed that my central sin is pride. In the right context, righteous pride gives me the confidence to assert what I believe. I have to be "proud" enough to trust that what I have to say is worthy of putting into a book! By contrast, inordinate pride draws me to seek admiration and attention for what I have to say.

Detachment is another example of twisted virtue. Detachment can lead to lack of compassion and neglect of others' needs. When my sinful detachment is healed, it gives me the capacity to step back from situations and see clearly what is right without being overpowered by emotions.

Signature sins are often strengths and gifts which have been tainted by the poison of sin. The serpent did not say to Eve, "Be bad and disobey God." He held out a promise. "You'll be wise. You'll know what

God knows. That is a very good thing." Like astigmatism, our vision is slightly distorted by sin. We look, but we see only in part. We think we are seeing clearly, but we are unaware of how much we are missing.

The apostle Paul wrote about the gifts of the Holy Spirit and urged his readers to seek after the most excellent way. He described the way sin distorts our vision, and he expressed longing for his own spiritual eyes to come fully open. "Now we see but a poor reflection as in a mirror; then we shall see face to face. Now I know in part; then I shall know fully, even as I am fully known" (1 Cor 13:12).

When we confess those distortions in our lenses, we ask for God's clarifying touch to restore what is corrupted by sin. When I pray, "Father, forgive me for my pride," I then add, "and teach me humility." When I confess my detachment, I ask God to help me love attachment. When I confess my gluttony and sloth, I pray for discipline and self-control. When God applies the antidote, my giftedness is allowed to shine through. I become more like Christ and more like who God created me to be.

The conviction of the Holy Spirit brings back sensation to deadened souls. As the feeling comes back, we begin to hurt. Pain tells us where the damage has been done and where to seek healing. As a psychotherapist I pay attention to where a person's emotional pain is located. Pain is the most reliable map to the place where God is at work in a person's life, and I want to participate in that work. Where there is pain, there is life and there is opportunity for healing.

NAMING THE ANTIDOTE

In his letter to churches, John assured his readers, "If we confess our sins, he is faithful and just and will forgive us our sins and purify us from all unrighteousness" (1 Jn 1:9). God desires us to be pure. He does not expect us to become pure on our own. He expects us to ask him to purify us.

Confession of sin begins the process of purification; even the hardest work is not effective without confession. Certainly we must work at changing; however, our human efforts will always be off-center. My aim will always be skewed when I try to correct my own sinfulness without God's guidance. If I could see straight, I wouldn't be in this predicament in the first place.

I recently read an interview with a public relations expert about celebrities who get caught in immorality (that's my word, not his). First they try to deny it. Then they try to ignore it and hope it will go away. Then they try to use power and influence to get the press called off. Finally they ask him, the PR expert, for help. He pointed out that celebrities who immediately and humbly acknowledge their misbehavior and ask for help recover their images much more swiftly. His recipe for PR success was "speed, humility, contrition and personal responsibility."

God's recipe for righteousness happens to also be good for public relations! The longer our sins remain hidden, the more difficult it is to root out the damage. The more quickly, humbly and penitently we acknowledge our sin, the more effectively the Lord can forgive us and cleanse us. Our signature sins can be transformed into the gifts and strengths that God intended them to be.

The naming of the antidote to our signature sin begins in quietness. In the previous chapter we focused on our resistance to facing the painful truth about ourselves. The practice of ascetic spiritual disciplines helps us clear away distractions. Silence and solitude allow us to listen to the conviction of the Holy Spirit. In quietness and solitude we can finally face those things inside ourselves that keep us from God.

Once we begin grappling with these truths, as millions of other believers in the great cloud of witnesses have done, we want to move on too rapidly. Perhaps you have even named your principle signature sin and have begun to practice quietly listening to God rather than filling your prayer time with words. It is important that you sit in this place for a good long while. Our temptation, once we have identified a problem, is to rush off to solve it. We want solutions. I must emphasize that contemplating our sin is not a small step to be quickly left behind as we move on to the rest of the task. This is the task! We do not solve the problem of sin once and for all. I will struggle with sin until the day I die.

Having said that, I must also say that if we remain stuck in the awareness of sin with no hope of progress, we will fall into despair. Confession of sin should be followed by asking God to bring about a transformation. We need to ask God to reveal the antidote. Just as there are no simple formulas for naming our signature sins, there are no shortcuts to receiving the name that God would give to the change he wants to bring about in our souls as he transforms us into the image of Christ.

SIGNATURE VIRTUES

Just as the names of our signature sins should be sought with prayer and help from someone who knows and loves us well, so also should we seek the names for our signature virtues. Just as the names of our central sins may leap immediately to mind, some of the corresponding virtues will be obvious. For example, humility is the virtue that should replace my signature sin of pride. As we saw for the names of sins, the name of our virtue will take on unique personal significance. When I ask for the antidote of humility to balance and transform my pride into accurate self-knowledge, I know exactly what humility will look like in my life.

One of my other signature sins is detachment. After pride, detachment was the second sin I felt the Holy Spirit leading me to name. Up until this point I had not told my wife about my new discipline of praying about my signature sins. After a week or two of confessing the sin of detachment and asking God to teach me to attach, my wife asked me, "What is going on? You are treating me differently." I explained what I had been praying for. She confirmed that God had indeed been answering my prayer.

Sometimes the name of the corrective virtue is not so obvious. One of my signature sins is anger. I hide it well; only my immediate family and long-term friends know it is there. I am seldom visibly agitated. After I came to name the signature sin of anger, I sought a name for the correcting virtue. I ran through the obvious alternatives: gentleness, patience, meekness and so forth. None of them fit exactly. They are wonderful virtues and I seek them in my life, but they don't provide the correction for the distortion of my personal anger. What I finally settled on, after much prayer, was the virtue of *surrender*. My anger flashes to the surface when someone or something thwarts my control in an area where I want control. The antidote, at least for my anger, is surrender.

My first clue about my antidote for anger should have been that I don't like the word *surrender!* Those virtues we are quickest to resist are usually the ones we most need. As Queen Gertrude said to Hamlet, "The lady doth protest too much, methinks." Our inordinate protesting spotlights our sin.

A dear friend and I have had several friendly arguments about detachment versus attachment. I argue for the first and she argues for the second. Both of us have had to acknowledge that our resistance reveals our need. It is no surprise that I was wounded in an early relationship by an inordinate, engulfing attachment, and she was wounded by an inordinate, withholding detachment. Each of us is right, of course, that our preference is an important virtue. Yet each of us needs the corrective influence of the one which makes us uncomfortable.

CORRECTIVE VIRTUES

Next we will turn to specific antidote virtues for signature sins. We can find ideas for naming virtues in many places, even in a thesaurus under the antonyms for the sins. Still nothing can replace the quiet voice of the Holy Spirit and a spiritual mentor in the process of naming antidotes for signature sins.

The antidote to pride is generally humility: being grounded in the simple unadorned reality of who we are. Humility takes different forms. If one's pride takes the form of vanity, modesty might be the corresponding antidote. Snobbery calls for the antidote of simplicity or poverty of spirit. Irreverence needs the antidote of reverence; disobedience needs obedience; impenitence needs penitence. Perfectionism as a form of pride might need to be corrected by grace or brokenness. Sentimentality could be countered with seriousness or simplicity. Presumption might call for the antidote of contrition.

Antidote names are often hard to take, like a bitter medicine. The word *submission* is unpopular in contemporary culture. For many people it brings up stereotypes of men's and women's roles. When authority is abused it is difficult to believe that submission to authority is a good thing. Nevertheless submission is an important antidote to combat pride, especially pride that takes the form of distrust.

I worked with one woman whose signature sin was pride. She named it selfishness. It was very difficult for her to acknowledge her selfishness because she had spent her life trying to pretend that she was not selfish. When she was a child her father had accused her of being selfish. She desperately wanted to shed this cruel label and sought every opportunity to disprove it. She was generous to a fault, sacrificing her own comforts for the good of others. She often allowed others to take advantage of her.

This woman had to learn that abstaining from openly selfish behaviors is not the same as eliminating selfishness. Gradually in the safety of psychotherapy she came to see that while much of her life was focused on giving to others, she had never truly given anything significant of herself to anyone else. Once she acknowledged to herself that selfishness had indeed taken hold of her life, she was able to begin to seek the antidote. For her the antidote was best named openness. She had kept herself closed off from others because she feared they would not care for her in the ways she wanted and felt she deserved. If she shared herself with others, she feared that she might become depleted. Also she was not sure she could trust others to meet her needs. Once she allowed some carefully chosen people to truly know her, she found that although no one else could care for her perfectly, the other rewards of openness and intimacy more than compensated for that loss.

Envy as a sin requires an antidote such as contentment, gratitude, joy or satisfaction. Jealousy will need to be countered with liberality, good will, kindness or abundance. The dangerous sin of malice will need to be combated with a strong fruit of the Spirit such as peace, kindness or gentleness. Contempt must be met with the counteracting virtues of love and generosity.

One patient who struggled with the sin of envy was always comparing herself to others. She lived in fear that she might be missing out on something good. She always felt inadequate and imagined that everyone else felt happy and complete. If she could just acquire some missing piece that she believed they had, she would finally be happy. Unfortunately the target of her envy was always changing. She might envy one person's financial means. If the next person to whom she compared herself was not financially well off, then they must certainly have a happier marriage. There was no limit to her creativity in finding something to envy about everyone.

I encouraged this woman to practice the discipline of thanksgiving. She began to list and journal about the good things in her life. She found it very difficult not to discount the good things in her own life. She had grown up feeling ashamed of her family, assuming that others were always judging her for belonging to such a raggedy bunch. Her envy began when as a child she desired the happy, normal families other children seemed to have. As she began to take stock of the good things in her own life, she also began to see others with different eyes. She could see that others had problems that weren't obvious from the outside. She could begin to be thankful for her own blessings without having to put them on a scale and compare them to the blessings of someone else.

Anger can come from many sources, some appropriate, some dangerous. If not carefully guarded, righteous anger can turn unrighteous. The antidote for anger needs to be named according to the most common source of the anger. For example, my anger is kindled when I do not have the control that I wish for. My antidote is surrender. Another person might feel the fire of anger when criticized and would need to pray for the antidote of humility. The sin of rage needs the antidote of peace, forbearance or harmony. Resentment should be countered with forgiveness and release. Pugnacity calls for the graciousness or tact. Retaliation calls for pardon. Paranoia should be met with trust.

The sin of anger causes many of the world's ills. It is a staple for any mental health professional. For many people the problem is their own anger. Others have been wounded by the anger of another. Usually the two go together. Those who are deeply angry have usually had plenty of anger dumped on them by someone significant in their lives.

One man who had been sadistically abused by his father vehemently denied that he struggled with anger, even though everyone close to him could see it. Once while we were talking about something his wife had done that displeased him, I asked him if they had fought over it. He looked at me as if I had accused him of something terrible. He said, "Of course we didn't fight over it. Do you think I would attack someone over something that small?" He equated anger of any kind with rage like that of his father.

While this man never acted in rage like his father, his anger always seethed below the surface. It sabotaged all his relationships because he cut off contact with anyone who wounded him. He was passive-aggressive in his marriage and believed that avoiding direct conflict was a virtue. All the while he was blind to the ways that his secret anger destroyed his relationships. For this man, as with many people, the expressions of anger were not usually sinful. Most often his anger started with legitimate grievances that come with every relationship. The sin came when he nursed the anger and allowed it to gradually erode the relationship. When he expressed the anger directly, he was able to release it. He needed to pray that God would teach him to speak his feelings. The antidote for his was not to eliminate anger but to be more direct and honest about it.

Often the sin of gluttony is best conquered with the antidote of self-discipline. Gluttony consists of wanting too much of a good thing. We do not want to say no to any appetite, whether for food, drink, television or any other pleasure. People who have been indulged often struggle with gluttony because no one ever taught them to say no to themselves. Those who have been deprived may also be gluttonous because they don't want to live under deprivation. Finding the antidote to gluttony requires addressing the specific desire which is the target of the gluttonous pleasure.

Food is the most common temptation for gluttony. Many people come to the awareness that they substitute food for some other lack in their life. One man came to see his gluttony in light of the ways that he kept every other appetite over-controlled. He was so disciplined and rigid in his exercise, cleanliness, work habits and spending that he found food to be his only indulgence. He would binge when he felt sad or lonely and then be tormented with guilt over his lack of self-control. The antidote to his gluttony was grace. When he began to allow himself to be imperfect and even messy without feeling undue guilt, his problem with bingeing began to diminish.

One young woman came to the realization that she overate and became obese because she was frightened of intimacy and sexuality. She was a sexual abuse survivor and, like many, feared that sexuality could only be abusive and painful. She was afraid to allow herself to be attractive to men or attracted by men. If any man showed an interest in her, she ran away. For her the antidote to gluttony was healthy desire. She began to journal whenever she was tempted to overeat. She found she was most tempted to overeat when she felt unwanted and began to open herself to desires, especially the wish for a romantic relationship. The fears associated with the desire to love and be loved made the whole prospect seem too risky. The fearful part of her squashed those desires by overeating and then hiding from others in shame. When she began to pray for the ability to desire without fear, she not only struggled less with gluttony, but others began to take notice of her, even before she lost weight. She began to enjoy her healthy desires and to satisfy those desires in healthy ways.

Lust is difficult to combat in a culture that promotes it in every imaginable way. Lust is most effectively opposed by the signature virtue of purity. Unchastity is countered by fidelity and chastity; immodesty is opposed by modesty. Prudery might be combated by playfulness or passion. Cruelty will need an antidote such as compassion or empathy.

People I know who have struggled with lust often benefit from tracking their times of greatest temptation. Lust is a perversion of the God-given desire to join with a soul mate. The desire for intimacy is healthy, but lust twists the desire. Many men I have worked with struggle most with lust when they feel out of control of their lives. Lust is possessive and power hungry. It turns people into objects of desire. Lust in this form is best dealt with by tackling its root issue, the hunger for control. I have worked with several men whose signature sin of lust weakened when they acknowledged their frustrations and feelings of powerlessness, whether at work or at home. If they dealt with their feelings directly, they were less tempted to take lustful power over another person in their hearts.

One woman's sin of lust took the form of using her sexuality to take power over men by presenting her physical beauty in a seductive way. She did not actually seek sexual contact; in fact she found sex rather frightening. She was living consistently with the message she had been taught, that women are sexual objects. She had been deeply wounded by both her culture and her family valuing sexuality above all else. Rather than let it be used against her, she learned to protect herself with the primary power she had. She thought her only options were to be victim or aggressor. For her the antidote to seductiveness was beauty. She began to learn to appreciate and accentuate her God-given inner and outer beauty without seductiveness. She had to learn to accept that some men would still view her as a sexual object regardless of how she presented herself, and that her worth came from God's love rather than from outward appearance.

Greed in the traditional form of avarice is best combated through generosity or liberality. Inordinate ambition may be counteracted by servanthood or sacrificiality. The sin of prodigality requires an antidote of discipline, self-sacrifice or simplicity. Stinginess may need a dose of faith in God's abundance; domination is best opposed by surrender or pacifism.

When I was a graduate student, one of my first patients was a young man who grew up in great wealth. His parents bought him a high-rise condominium in the most prestigious part of the city and paid all his expenses while he went to school to enter the family business. He was conflicted about his future and had become depressed and anxious. He entered counseling to sort out his life and his priorities. When we began meeting, it quickly became clear that he felt the desire to take his life in a different direction than his parents would want. He wanted to go into some kind of Christian service and make an impact on the world through serving the underserved. His friends affirmed his desire and he felt clear that God was calling him in that direction. What kept him frozen was that if he pursued the life he wanted, he knew his parents would withdraw their financial support. He could make a living without their help, but not enough for his accustomed lifestyle. After several weeks of sorting through the choices, he concluded that the sacrifice was not worth it. His love of money held him too tightly. He returned to pursue his parents' dream for his life.

The signature sin of sloth, neglect of spiritual responsibilities, is best resisted through the pursuit of the virtues of zeal and diligence. When sloth takes the form of laziness, the antidote might be discipline, commitment, ambition or willingness. Indifference is countered through the virtues of concern, enthusiasm, interest, passion or involvement. A person who seeks to confront the sin of cowardice should ask God to impart courage, boldness or conviction. Sadness, sinful when it becomes an addiction, is best confronted through seeking after hope, optimism and joy.

Sloth is one of the most discouraging sins to confront. Sloth is the very antithesis of confrontation of sin. In the face of sin, sloth simply looks away. As a psychotherapist I have many stories of people who faced the sin of sloth. Unfortunately, many of the stories have no definite conclusion. I see people take a few steps on the path of spiritual formation and self-discovery, only to drop out when the work gets too difficult. People whose signature sin is sloth often ask for help in their spiritual formation when they are in pain. They want to do only enough work to get out from under the pain and get back to being comfortable. They do not feel challenged to move on to the next stage of development, so they often stagnate.

Sloth wants others to be responsible and waits for someone else to do the work. The slothful person may even seek help from others, asking for accountability. The danger is that the others may begin to take greater interest in the individual's spiritual growth than he or she is taking. Sloth requires internal motivation to change. Such motivation comes from the conviction of the Holy Spirit and not from sheer determination.

I worked with an adolescent who struggled with sloth. She did not want to do the hard work of facing the painful losses in her past. She used drugs and partying to turn off the pain. Her sloth was primarily related to hidden anger and sadness because her father had left her and her mother. She feared that the sadness would overwhelm her and that anger would destroy what little relationship she had with her emotionally distant father. Journaling became this young woman's antidote to sloth. Whenever she began to get depressed and was tempted to escape into substance use or partying, I would ask her what she was angry about. She could seldom articulate her feelings out loud; however she could pour them out at the tip of a pen. Then she would feel restored and be able to reengage in her life.

Slothful people have difficulty doing what needs to be done when it needs to be done. They need discipline and routine. They find success if they adopt regular scheduled habits which remove the repeated decision to act. If they fall away from their routine, they will begin to slip.

Very often people I have seen for counseling in the past will make an appointment for a "check up." They acknowledge that they have slipped away from the patterns we established for their spiritual and mental health and they need help reestablishing the routine. A daily time of devotion is helpful. I have found the season of Lent to be a powerful antidote to the sin of sloth. Regardless of the state of my spiritual life, Lent provides a call to self-examination and discipline. Because I am joined by others who are also observing Lent, I have greater support and accountability in my disciplines.

I noted earlier that fear is a sin when it should have been dispelled by our experience of God; in some ways fear is the heart of all sin. Some people live their lives crippled by fear. Their fears usually have clear and understandable roots; they were realistic at some point. When God has proven himself faithful, however, fear should lessen its hold over us. Fear becomes sinful when we let it lead us away from the path of spiritual formation which God has laid out for us.

I have known many people whose signature sin is fear. One woman acknowledged that fear laced itself through every moment in her life.

I could empathize with her fear; her life had given her many reasons to live braced for the next wave that would knock her off her feet. She gradually came to see that in all those waves God had always proven faithful. Even the worst times in her life had been redeemed. God had always been present, even if she hadn't realized it. As she learned to relax and breathe, both literally and figuratively, and lean into the waves, she found that God's grace was sufficient to sustain her through everything life threw at her. Her antidote to fear was trust.

So far, in all these stories of signature sins which people have named, confronted and countered with virtues, the common theme is that the sufferers did not go into battle alone. In the next chapter we will explore how human relationships help us grow in our intimacy with God.

🌀

TAMING YOUR WAYWARD HEART

- Try this contemplative exercise. Set aside an hour for silence in a comfortable, private place. Spend several minutes quieting and centering your heart. Repeating the Jesus prayer can be helpful: *Lord Jesus Christ, Son of the Living God, have mercy on me, a sinner.* Quietly reading Scripture can be helpful as well, but try not to fill your mind with ideas or words. This is not a time to talk to God, but to listen. When you have stilled yourself, sit silently and open your heart to whatever God might want to say to you. If it is difficult for you to be silent without words, try meditating on a single word or short phrase such as "God is good." The author of *The Cloud of Unknowing* speaks of directing our "naked intent" toward God and not trying to control the process. If distractions, problems or things you need to do pop into your mind, jot them down to attend to later. Imagine gently lifting them up to God, then go back to silent listening. Journal about your experience.

- If total silence is too difficult for you, a different kind of contemplative exercise might work better. Try setting aside an extended period of time to do nothing but listen to beautiful music. Pick something evocative, preferably with no words or with words in a language you don't know. Classical music is particularly effective, although it may be best to listen to a piece with which you are not familiar. A requiem mass can be quite powerful for this purpose. Listen to it uninterrupted and undistracted by other tasks. Imagine that you are simply sitting with God enjoying this part of his creation together. Journal about your experience.

- How are silence and solitude for you?

   When you try to spend time alone, what feelings do you become aware of?

- Meditate on Hebrews 11:13-16.

   In what ways might God be calling you to leave a comfortable familiar place and long for a heavenly country?

- Look up your signature sin(s) in a Bible concordance. What is said throughout Scripture about your signature sin?

   How does this contribute to the antidotes offered in this chapter?

- Try meditating on longing. With eyes closed, listen to a song about longing for heaven. Imagine what heaven will be like. How does such an experience change your day?

10

Formation in Community

SPIRITUAL FORMATION AND LASTING CHANGE are difficult outside of a supportive Christian community. While spiritual formation certainly takes place in our own private relationship with God, we were designed to thrive in community. We are made in the image of the God of love, and God's image is reflected in our need to be in relationship with him and with each other.

I have been blessed to be part of several healthy communities. I grew up in a church that served as an extended family. That church was part of a small town where most people either knew me or knew someone in my immediate family. Since then I've been a part of several churches and work environments with many of the qualities of a caring community. For more than a decade I have been part of a small group that meets every two weeks.

I have come to take community for granted, and I am frequently jarred back to reality when I consult with people who do not belong to any community at all. There is no loneliness like that of a person who feels no one on earth would notice if he or she disappeared. Some people feel they have to pay someone to be their friend. I've worked with couples who have absolutely no friends, including each other. The marriage stays stable because living with someone you hate can feel better than being absolutely alone. Being in a community does not guarantee immunity to loneliness. Many people feel alone even within a community. Perhaps they know people in their church by name but never have anything like an intimate conversation with anyone.

Healthy communities promote healing. People who are in healthy communities tend to be healthier themselves. Healthy communities put us in contact with people who can care for us, and they give us opportunities to care for others.

Many people who come to a psychotherapist could have been helped by a caring layperson if one had only been available. For that reason I believe in training skilled natural helpers in the art of lay counseling. Research consistently shows that for the normal stresses of life, a caring layperson is just as effective as a mental health professional in bringing about healing.

COMMUNITY AS CRUCIBLE

Although the Fall has left us disconnected, God created human beings to be communal. The New Testament refers to the church as a body. Besides his lengthy passage on the body of Christ in 1 Corinthians 12:12-27, Paul wrote this concise statement about the body: "Just as each of us has one body with many members, and these members do not all have the same function, so in Christ we who are many form one body, and each member belongs to all the others" (Rom 12:4-5).

Years ago I read Dietrich Bonhoeffer's book *Life Together*. It has deeply influenced my thoughts about what the church can and can't be. Bonhoeffer pointed out that true Christian community is nothing like our fantasies and illusions of a wonderful, welcoming family. Sometimes it is like that, but more often the church is like a crucible. We have to live in proximity to people we don't like. Even if we do like them in the beginning, we will soon discover their annoying qualities.

The crucible of a community heats us up and holds us in so we can't get away. In the process it refines us, bringing our impurities to the surface where they can be skimmed away. Even the desert fathers and mothers, many of whom lived as hermits in caves, settled near each other and created the first model for the communal life of monasteries. They recognized that community is necessary for spiritual purification.

On our own we easily ignore our own sharp edges. When we live close to other people, we constantly bump up against each other, and our unfinished edges are impossible to hide. "As iron sharpens iron, / so one person sharpens another" (Prov 27:17 TNIV). If we are serious about confronting our own signature sins, we should seek to be part of a community where this kind of sharpening can take place.

NEITHER MAYBERRYS NOR HOLLERS

Urban and suburban dwellers mistakenly think that small towns are either idyllic Mayberrys or backward hollers for ignorant hicks. One stereotype about small towns is true: they offer far less anonymity than the city. In small communities, for good or bad, people know each other's business. People also know each other's history. There are fewer secrets in small communities.

The negative side of everybody knowing everybody else is the sense that you can never escape your reputation or your family's reputation, and you must keep an ear open for gossip about yourself. On the positive side, you have the assurance that the people around you are both supporting you and holding you accountable.

Today an economic tourniquet is systematically choking off resources from rural areas and concentrating them in urban centers. As a result, the influence of small rural communities is disappearing from our culture. The decline comes with psychological costs to rural people. I direct a not-for-profit organization, the Center for Rural Psychology, with a mission of more effectively meeting the needs of people in small communities.

The decline of rural communities obviously affects rural people themselves. What is less obvious is how the decline affects the rest of the nation. At one time in our history most people had some connection to rural life. In the 1920s one-third of the U.S. population lived on small farms. By the 1990s it was less than 2 percent of the U.S. population. In under one hundred years we have gone from a primarily rural culture to a society clustered in a few urban areas.

Small-town values are the backbone of our culture, but fewer and fewer people experience small town life. Some corporations still recruit heavily in rural areas because they find that young people there have a stronger work ethic. More than 40 percent of military recruits—and our war dead—come from small towns.

I don't want to promote inaccurate images of rural America. It is no utopia. What can be said for sure about small towns is that people have to learn to live with their neighbors.

NED'S BOY

As a child I was very conscious that I was not anonymous. Once I went to the grocery store for my mother. I realized in the checkout line that I had forgotten to bring a check to pay for the groceries. I asked the checker if I could leave the groceries for a few minutes while I went home to get some money. She studied my face for a moment and then said, "You're Ned's boy, aren't you?" I confirmed that I was Ned's boy. She sent me home with the groceries and said I could bring the money back later.

I enjoy many aspects of suburban life. I have a multitude of choices for entertainment, dining and cultural activities. I even have hundreds of churches within driving distance. It would be very easy, however, to live in the suburbs and never put down roots.

Many of my patients have no friendships, even at work. They have no church community, or else they have church-hopped too many times to maintain any ties. Some go to churches with thousands of others and don't recognize another person at the worship service. They live in sprawling housing developments where every house looks like its neighbor and the average length of stay is about three years.

My wife and I have chosen to stay at the same church for the entire time we have lived in our present home. We know the neighbors on our block. Our friendships here span almost two decades. You can create community in the suburbs—if you want to and you know how. In a small town you have no choice. You would have to work hard to *not* be part of the community. Even if you isolate yourself and seldom venture outdoors, people still know who you are, and they know whom to call if they don't seen any activity at your home for awhile.

I am not suggesting that communities in small rural towns are healthier or happier than communities in urban and suburban areas. What I am saying is that for most people in our culture anonymity is the default condition; community is an option. People in cities and suburbs have to *choose* to be in a community. They have to find one or start one and actively seek to be part of it. If things don't go well in that community, they can always leave it and join another one without even changing jobs or houses.

Community and Sin

What does all of this have to do with sin? Anonymity and the diffusion of responsibility create a place for sin to flourish. Sin does not thrive under accountability. While communities are not always healthy and do not always confront sin, it is difficult to combat sin in the absence of any community at all. Jesus was clear in his instructions to us: take care of each other, especially watch over the weakest and most vulnerable, do not ignore the importance of gathering together, appreciate each other's gifts, and hold each other accountable. In other words, be the church.

Christ calls us as individuals to take up our crosses and follow him.

But Christ also calls us as communities to bear one another's burdens and live in harmony. The immediate response of Jesus' followers after his crucifixion was to come together. The book of Acts follows the activities of the church learning to be the church after Jesus' resurrection. The Christian life is not only one of personal piety but also of communion. Though many of us might be called to the desert, literally or figuratively, to fast and pray, few of us are called to live there. Most of us face the more difficult task of learning to live with and love our neighbors.

Christian community should be the place where we learn to be more like Christ; where we are transformed into his image from the inside out. Instead many churches have become places where we learn to polish our own images. The arrangement is upside down. My personal piety should draw me toward Christ; the church should help me integrate and deepen my transformation. Instead, churches are sometimes transformed into sparkling store windows designed to draw people in and keep them entertained and happy with the product. Certainly the church should be a winsome and welcoming presence in our world. There should be a balance between sinking into sullenness and propping up superficial cheerfulness.

LIKE-MINDED PEOPLE

Every Christian who seeks to grow in righteousness needs a community to foster that growth. *Community* does not always mean *congregation*. Ideally the body of believers with whom we worship will help us practice penitent self-examination. Even if they do not, we can search out a group of like-minded people who hunger for a more radical kind of honesty. For several decades the small group movement has opened opportunities for Christians to have something like what first-century Christians enjoyed: small, intimate families of believers who support and sustain each other in Christian formation.

For me, two different types of spiritual formation groups stand out as exceptional models. One is Renovaré, the organization established and guided by Richard Foster, which seeks to introduce the contemporary church to the writings and practices of the church throughout its earlier history. The other is the spiritual direction group, introduced by the Shalem Institute.

In *A Spiritual Formation Workbook: Small-Group Resources for Nurturing Christian Growth*, Renovaré provides a practical and profound introduction to the spiritual life. Renovaré promotes the premise that the Christian spiritual life can be divided into six streams modeled after the life of Jesus and the key traditions of church history. The six streams of tradition are the Contemplative, the Holiness, the Charismatic, the Social Justice, the Evangelical and the Incarnational. In the next chapter we will more fully explore the streams.

My wife and I and several other people started a small group using *A Spiritual Formation Workbook* when it was first published. The early stages of a group are always important for setting the tone. Groups are usually made up of a mix of temperaments. Some people want intense intimacy, some people want light socializing, some people want to read and study something together, some people want to spend much time praying. The Renovaré model strikes a wonderful balance of different needs and desires. It helps group members foster intimacy with questions and discussion. The workbook provides practical ways for believers to grow in spiritual formation and ways they can support and hold each other accountable in spiritual growth.

The small group that we started more than a decade ago is still going. It is unreasonable to expect every small group to turn into this kind of community, but when it happens, it is a blessing. Our group has gone through changes as some people have moved away and others have joined. We have seen each other through the deaths of seven parents, and we have celebrated several children's weddings. Twice over the years we have returned to the book that helped us get started and found that it renewed our thinking. We go through dry periods when we are too busy to meet regularly, and we have arguments about what our group should be doing. Those are all elements which make up a community.

The other type of group that I have found exciting is the spiritual direction group, introduced by the Shalem Institute. In Rose Mary Dougherty's book *Group Spiritual Direction: Community for Discernment*, she presents a model of prayerful groups focused on periods of silent listening to God on each other's behalf. These groups are not social gatherings but are focused intensely on discerning God's still, small voice in the confusion of daily living. They go beyond the role of individual spiritual direction to add the discerning ears of several people in the group rather than just one director. My wife and I have taught the method of this group in several contexts, and students have gone on to establish groups of their own. The groups can be ongoing or they can meet for a specified period of time, such as six months, before coming to an end.

My wife and I were part of this type of group spiritual direction for several years. Like our spiritual formation group, our spiritual direction group became a community. There we sometimes confronted each other and talked about our own personal struggles with sin. The difference was that the spiritual direction group was less socially involved with each other and more focused on prayer and discernment. Our group could sometimes pray silently together for hours. There is something intimate and powerful about sitting together in prayerful silence. It was wonderful to be together in Christ's presence without having to talk, sing or pray out loud.

Both the spiritual direction group and the spiritual formation group provided a place to talk honestly and vulnerably about our relationship with God. By participating in each other's spiritual lives, each of us saw other ways of relating to God, and we enjoyed the privilege of seeing God at work in each other. We could be imperfect together. Several of us live far from our families, so we could be family to each other. Over the years conflicts, tensions and annoyances arose. One group is still going; the other came to a natural point where it was time to end. I consider myself blessed to have had these two groups in my life. Both have been instrumental in my spiritual growth.

MAKING COMMUNITY SAFE

I am sad that few people get to experience such long-term intimacy and stability. A group must be intentional about seeking this kind of honesty. Few congregations are safe enough or intimate enough to provide the space for growth which a small group can provide. Even then, someone in the group must take the first step.

Pastors have asked me how to help their congregations become safe places where people can acknowledge to each other their struggles with sin. I reply that the pastors and the elders should publicly acknowledge their own struggles with sin. When the most powerful and respected members of the community show this kind of vulnerability, it becomes safe for everyone to do so.

I witnessed the power of vulnerability in church leadership at a church where I was invited to lead a men's retreat about the struggle with pornography. This group of African American men listened to the statistics and realities of pornography and became powerfully convicted. The pastor and several elders confessed their struggles with the temptations of pornography. Their honesty made it safe for every man there to acknowledge his own battle. That morning became a catalyst for a revival of sorts as the pastor started a series of sermons on the danger of sexual sins. The leaders' honesty and courage paved the way for others to follow, and I am confident that it affected the life of every member of the church.

A COMMUNITY OF TWO

Not only in groups can we find a safe place to share our struggles. Everyone can benefit from what many have called a soul friend.

In recent years the art of spiritual direction has enjoyed a revival. Spiritual direction is a form of relationship in which one person plays a key role in the spiritual formation of another person. Spiritual direction can be formal or informal. Some people attend training programs where they are instructed and supervised in the practice of spiritual direction. They may receive a graduate degree or certificate in spiritual formation. Other people are simply sought out by others for spiritual mentoring because of their maturity and wisdom.

Spiritual direction can be a helpful companion to psychotherapy. In psychotherapy the focus is usually on one's relationship patterns and problems of living at home, at work, at school and so forth. In spiritual direction the focus of the time together is primarily on one's relationship with God. While the two practices overlap, the goals are different. For example, in my psychotherapeutic work with a person we may talk about how their relationship with their father affected their feelings toward God. In spiritual direction the relationship with God is likely to be the central theme of most sessions.

I once worked with a man whose father was cruel and sadistic. His father was also extremely religious. When this patient described God he talked of a distant, scowling God ready to condemn him at every turn. This patient's father had distorted every area of his life, including his relationship with God. As we worked through his pain and anger in all areas of his life, his relationship with God was among the things that changed.

Let me contrast that counseling experience with my experience of being in spiritual direction. My spiritual director and I began and ended every session in silence and prayer. During the session we talked about my prayer life. We explored the different spiritual disciplines that I practiced and what areas were a struggle for me. We would talk about an upcoming spiritual retreat or something that my director wanted me to contemplate. In short the entire session was directly related to my relationship with God. Spiritual direction usually occurs less frequently than psychotherapy, perhaps monthly.

How does one choose a spiritual director or mentor? The simplest answer is that we should choose someone that we want to become like. If we see Christlikeness in another person, it is natural to want to follow the same path that person has trod. The prospective spiritual director should evidence the fruit of the Spirit: love, joy, peace, patience, kindness, goodness, faithfulness, gentleness and self-control. Because listening will be the mentor's primary role, pay the greatest attention to the person's ability to listen, not to his or her ability to say wise things. Finally, the person you seek should not be overly eager to be your spiritual mentor. Those spiritually ready for the role are often the most reticent. The person should take on the role only with soberness and prayer.

Stone Soup

Pastors who understand the importance of healing communities face a perplexing paradox. If you create a church that is a safe and healing community, people will flock to it. At that point the congregation often flounders. Those who were providing for the needs of a few hurting people are suddenly asked to head up ministries that reach out to many more, a task that might not fit their gifts. For this and other reasons, it is not wise for us to put our hopes for true Christian community in churches and pastors, especially in urban and suburban areas where a church's potential size is almost unlimited. Pastors and congregations can facilitate healthy communities for spiritual formation, but they cannot be the sole source of community.

As I draw this chapter to a close I have the guilty feeling that I have just told a crowd of starving people that there are feasts out there somewhere, if they can only find them. I don't want to give that impression. Communities are not unearthed; they are created.

The image of people starving for community reminds me of the folk tale about the soldier who made stone soup. The soldier was traveling alone during a famine and came to a small town. He asked where he could find a place to sleep and a meal. The villagers, jealously guarding their meager stocks of food, told him there was no food in the village and he had best move on. He confidently replied that he did not need any handouts and would make himself a batch of delicious stone soup.

The soldier ceremoniously borrowed a large cauldron, filled it with water and set the water to boil. He then cleaned and dropped in a large stone and casually commented, within earshot of the curious onlookers, that although plain stone soup was certainly adequate, stone soup with onions was far superior. One inquisitive villager, eager to try the concoction, ran home to retrieve some onions. This scene repeated itself as the soldier commented that stone soup was far tastier with cabbage, then potatoes, then beef and so on. We know where the story ends. By sharing their meager resources, everyone in the village, including the hungry soldier, shared a wholesome meal.

The formation of every community requires someone to initiate it. When surrounded by people who insist they have nothing to share, it takes faith to start a big pot of stone soup. In my experience most people are hungry for community, even if they are also wary of joining one.

I teach in a master's program in clinical psychology. The program lasts two years. The faculty of the program tries to facilitate an environment where the cohort of students who will spend two years together can form a strong and healthy community. The sad reality, of course, is that the community must dissolve at the end of two years. Some years the cohort forms a healthy cohesive community; sometimes it is not as successful. In any case, in the crucible of this temporary community people are transformed. Although people promise to stay in touch, the community will never again exist in the form it has taken over the previous two years.

I usually give a challenge to the graduating students. They have experienced a community that we as faculty have helped them create. They now have a responsibility to go out and do likewise. They cannot wait for someone else to create a community for them. They need to start one. Some communities, like the student cohort, will not last as long as they like. Others may be long term. But someone always needs to get out a pot and start boiling water.

I hope the reader will accept the same challenge I give to the graduating students. If you are longing for a group of people who can walk together and share a part of each other's journeys, give out some invitations. Ask God to bring some people to mind. You might be amazed at who God picks. You never know who will have some of the most flavorful ingredients to add to your soup! Through community we find others who have resources that we lack. My community holds up before me a mirror which helps me see how I need to change in order to become more Christlike. My community also supports and encourages me as I strive in that direction.

6

TAMING YOUR WAYWARD HEART

- How far back in your family tree do you need to look to find people who lived in the same place for more than one generation?

  How has generational stability or instability of place affected you spiritually?

- Are you in community right now? Do you have roots? Journal about the thoughts, feelings and images that come to mind when you think about community.

- Make a map of your community. Put yourself as a circle in the middle of the page, then draw circles for each of the people in your community, placing the people closer or farther away from your circle according to the closeness of your relationships.

    Do you find certain areas of greater community and areas of less community?

    What trends do you notice?

- How have you been wounded by community?

    What fears are raised by the thought of committing yourself to community?

- Can the church meet our needs for community?

    What is your image of a healthy Christian community?

    In what ways is your vision realistic or unrealistic?

- If you find community lacking in your life, are you willing to create a community? Consider starting a community for the purpose of spending a limited period of time together. Don't begin with any assumption that the group will last beyond an agreed-upon period of time. If you use a book such as this one or the *Spiritual Formation Workbook* mentioned in the chapter, the number of chapters might provide a convenient length for the group. Spread the word of your group to your pastor(s) and others in leadership in your church.

11

Spiritual Rhythms
of Sin and Grace

WHEN CHRIST CALLS ME TO FOLLOW HIM, I have only a moment to make up my mind. Such moments reveal my character.

If my loves are properly ordered, I will abandon trivial comforts with no hesitation and follow Christ. I will sell all I own to purchase the field where I have found the treasure or to purchase the pearl of great price (Mt 13:44-45). I will sell all my possessions and give to the poor and follow Christ (Mt 19:16-30; Mk 10:17-31). Jesus is not referring to material possessions alone but to status, image, safety, comfort, entertainment and every other good thing we make into an idol. At the moment when Jesus beckons, we have the opportunity to leave it all and follow him. If I truly believe God is good, I won't hesitate. If I am unsure of God, the moment will pass me by.

Trusting God is not a once and for all decision. Jesus does not knock at our door only once in our lives. He is not content that we once gave ourselves to him. He asks us to follow him every day.

Human beings are created not to stay put but to go on pilgrimage. We follow God to a particular place where we might rest for a while and even see a new miracle like water coming from a rock. Eventually

God says, "OK. Pack it up. Let's move on."

God is always calling us to grow and change and move on to another level of spiritual maturity. The direction I am to go next is not always clear. Sometimes I have to follow God in a direction which seems entirely wrong. I have to trust that he is good.

WINDING ROADS

In the Big Sky Country of Montana where I grew up, anything that towers above the prairie can be seen for miles. You might set out to aim for a landmark such as a butte, a radio tower or a mountain. The country roads, however, are seldom laid out in a straight line. Many began as wagon trails and they wind around natural obstacles like hills, valleys, lakes and streams. The ultimate destination is visible in the distance, but the traveler must sometimes turn and go in the opposite direction. At that point the route does not make sense. Although the destination is clear, the route to get there is not direct. The traveler must suspend doubts and must trust that eventually the road will head in the right direction again.

In the monastic traditions, the spiritual life was understood to follow a straight or linear path. A person left the common life and entered the religious life. The early years in the monastery were the *purgative* stage when the disciple broke free from the material attachments of this world. The disciple then entered into the *illuminative* phase of seeing God's truth more clearly and through new eyes. Some finally entered into the *unitive* stage of deep union with God, having been purified to the point of being able to see him clearly. Over the course of years the monk's path went from point A to point B to point C.

The linear model is valuable for understanding stages of our spiritual lives even outside religious orders. In everyday life, however, most of us find that spiritual life does not move forward in a straight line. I experience periods of growth followed by periods of stagnation or even periods of backsliding. Sometimes I feel that I am back at square one or off on a side track irrelevant to my final destination. At other times I feel that I've accelerated to a new level. Often I feel that I have waited and am still waiting endlessly for God to show up and do anything at all.

Most of us have had the experience of facing some inner flaw such as a signature sin and feeling disappointed that we are back where we started. In frustration we say "I thought I had already dealt with that." In reality we are not back at exactly the same place. We are dealing with the same issue, but from a different level of maturity.

We can think of spiritual growth not as a linear progression but as a cyclical process. It resembles a journey around a mountain. I come back to the same side of the mountain and see what is essentially the same view, except that now I see it from a different height and with greater clarity. Our growth is cyclical like that. It is not a ladder but a winding staircase. It is not a straight line but more like a helix. We need to purge our house of idols not once but repeatedly throughout our lives.

If we take the stages of spiritual development—*purgation, illumination* and *union*—and turn them in a circle, we get a picture of the cycle of spiritual development. Something abruptly breaks us out of the complacency of the common life. God may directly and miraculously intervene and speak to us. Such unmistakable moments cut right through the mundane. More often God uses the normal crises, annoyances, losses and hard knocks of life to get our attention. Whatever the source of the interruption, we become aware that things are not as they should be. We respond by taking a step out of comfort and toward Christ. We enter into the stage of purgation.

Purgation: Letting Go

Purgation is characterized by awakened longings. At the moment of choice we know that our loves and our lives are not properly ordered.

They are out of alignment with the divine. We hunger to bring the disordered to order, though we fear what it will cost us.

Purgation begins when we decide it is more appealing to follow Christ than to stay comfortable. When we enter the wilderness of purgation, we don't know how long the journey will be. We step out in faith with no intention to return.

In the purgative stage we discard along the trail those things to which we have clung. It is important to let go of those weights without being able to see what lies ahead. If I could see the Promised Land from Egypt, I would not need faith to enter the wilderness. While we travel we have to take our comfort from God's presence rather than from our old addictions. That is the point of going through the wilderness—to prove that God is sufficient to meet our needs.

Because I am not a good swimmer, I sometimes imagine purgation as floating in water far from shore. I would grab every piece of debris that came along to try to keep myself afloat. I would forget that in the beginning I was clinging to a pillar sunk deep into the ocean floor. Floating debris has obscured my sure foundation. If I let it all go, that which cannot save me will float away and that which is permanent will remain. I have to let go to find out that God is still there and still good.

This purging process can take a long time or it can take only a few moments. It is entirely up to me. If I am stubborn and release one item at a time, the process will be slow. If I surrender and let it all go, the process could happen very quickly.

Purgation could also be called disillusionment. God strips away our illusions. The word implies pain. When we are disillusioned we have lost something, and we have not yet received anything to replace it.

In *The Dark Night of the Soul*, a classic in the contemplative literature, the sixteenth-century monk John of the Cross described the journey of a soul that seeks after union with God. In this lifelong quest there are two dark nights of cleansing that confront the pilgrim along the way.

The first comes after the purgative stage; the second follows the illumi-native stage. The two times of purgation correspond to the dual nature of humans, spiritual and sensual. The second cleansing, the dark night of the spirit or soul, is most well known. John points out that only the most mature believers encounter the dark night of the soul after a life set apart for singular service to God. The first and far more prevalent dark night is the night of the senses, that is, of the emotions.

John of the Cross asserts that every seeker after God will come to the purgation of the senses because every pilgrim begins the journey with emotional cravings. The hungers of the flesh divert the believer from a deeper union with God. The soul that is still addicted to the flesh cannot surrender to spiritual intimacy with God. The dark night of the senses is a sort of detoxification, a period of necessary withdrawal. Though it is painful, it is a sign of maturity that God has deemed the soul ready for this step. John likened it to the weaning of an infant that is ready for solid food. Purgation comes when the believer has matured to the point of readiness for spiritual meat rather than spiritual milk (Heb 5:13-14).

John of the Cross and other spiritual writers speak of the hold that sensuality has on us, referring to the perceived need for pleasure and comfort, especially in the spiritual life. Excitement and joy character-ize the first love of a person in a new relationship with Christ. There is danger in expecting the spiritual life to stay that way.

The honeymoon stage of a marriage is full of passion and excitement, but a healthy marriage needs to grow deeper roots beneath the surface feel-ings so it can survive life's storms. The spiritual life needs deeper roots to sustain it beyond superficial times of pleasure. The disciple must broaden the definition of what a close relationship with God feels like.

In the early years of marriage I recall a sort of silly excitement after our first big fights. We shared a kind of intimacy after a healthy, non-abusive argument that was more complex and satisfying than the more superficial forms of closeness. After a good fight, both of us felt greater trust in each other. All the same it was an unsettling and frightening time. Each of us got a new and unexpected glimpse of the other. Suddenly the other person was unfamiliar. At this stage of a marriage each partner goes from feeling like the other person is all I've ever wanted in a mate to an experience of mysterious otherness that I can't fully comprehend and I'm not sure I like.

In the same way, our relationship with God must grow beyond simple innocent first romance. In order for the relationship to deepen, it must become more complex. We must face the vast and mysterious otherness of God.

John of the Cross used Job as an example of a deepening experience of God. While Job's wife and friends despaired that Job's relationship with God could ever be repaired, Job persisted and doggedly hung onto his faith. Ultimately Job expressed disappointment with God. Then God came down to have a face-to-face conversation with him. While the encounter was terrifying, John of the Cross points out that it was also intimate in a way few humans have ever experienced.

Like Job's friends, many well-meaning people inadvertently discourage the believer who is experiencing a healthy transition into the purgative stage of spiritual development. Too many people believe that the spiritually mature person should always feel happy, healthy and successful. We think that if someone is suffering, the person must somehow deserve it. If people around us affirm a negative perspective as Job's friends did, we can lose sight of our trust in God's goodness.

God's motives for withdrawing from us are far from fickle or cruel. Like a father calling his toddler to take the first steps, God moves a few steps down the road and calls us to follow. By leading us into the desert he expresses his confidence in our readiness to enter a more mature kind of relationship with him. He knows the perfect time when we have grown to the point that we are ready to be stretched further. Every step of growth comes with its own unique temptation to step in a direction away from our Father's outstretched arms, but he does not allow us to be tempted beyond what we are able to endure (1 Cor 10:13).

For the soul in the dark night of the senses, spiritual weaning does not feel like progress. When we let go of the familiar and comfortable we feel sadness, even if what we are gaining is better than what we have abandoned. People who have experienced cruelty or abandonment at the hands of their parents find it hard to believe that a good God would withdraw from them or allow them to experience pain.

Spiritual formation requires us to grow in our capacity to distinguish between the healthy pain of growth and the unhealthy pain caused by sin. When we quiet our minds and bodies enough to hear God's still small voice, we will experience the pain of seeing how our sins lead us away from our Father's arms. Healthy pain awakens our longing to draw closer to him.

Even in the sixteenth century, John of the Cross discerned the difference between clinical depression, what he called a melancholic temperament, and the appropriate spiritual mourning that comes with purgation from sensual attachments. Depression is characterized by lack of progress toward maturity. Mourning, on the contrary, is productive; its tears are fruitful.

ILLUMINATION: THE VIEW FROM THE MOUNTAINTOP

A pilgrim in the purgative stage struggles with the temptation to cling to illusions rather than look for the truth. Once God strips away the illusions, darkness evaporates and the world appears in a new light. Old familiar things look shiny and new. We all know the excitement of such mountaintop experiences. After we have trudged up a long and difficult hill, the clouds suddenly clear away and we feel like we can see forever. We forget the difficulty of the climb as we gaze about at the new vista.

Believers who are in the illuminative stage typically encounter resistance from the people who knew them before. Once we are enlightened, we see how old habits and old ways of thinking imprisoned us. Meanwhile our friends and family still cling to those same illusions which once deceived us. Relationships can be strained and even broken if others do not accept our abandonment of illusions.

When Jesus reclined at table with prostitutes, lepers and tax collectors, even his disciples had trouble releasing their viewpoint that such people are untouchable. At those times Jesus appeared to be a heretic. Saul had to be struck blind on the road to Damascus for Jesus to get his attention. When the scales fell from his eyes Saul became Paul, the friend of his former enemies and the enemy of his former friends.

Not everyone who claims to be enlightened actually sees with new eyes. Throughout history many people have falsely claimed to receive new revelations from God. Some were lying, but others believed their own mistaken claims.

As a result of the Fall, we are all born into a world where life constantly requires us to discern truth from falsehood. We cannot always trust our perceptions. Our sinful hearts distort the truth in self-serving ways.

The pilgrim's journey through the wilderness requires constant choices of which direction to take. Without God to align our vision, we will go off course. The wrong road will look wider, more appealing and more in line with the final destination. Jesus warned about the promise of an apparently easier path. "Enter through the narrow gate. For wide is the gate and broad is the road that leads to destruction, and many enter through it. But small is the gate and narrow the road that leads to life, and only a few find it" (Mt 7:13-14).

Even those pilgrims who enter the illuminative stage have not arrived at perfection. Their sight is clearer but it is not perfect. Naive to the dangers of the new place, they can still wander off the true path.

For this reason the Christian church has always required more than an individual's excitement to test the truth of a new vision. We can err at both extremes, either refusing to receive a prophetic word or abandoning orthodoxy for a false new gospel.

There is constant tension at the point of intersection between acknowledgment of God's prophetic call and the similar call from the great deceiver. Those who encountered Jesus wanted him to give them nice clear rules to distinguish between the two. Better yet, they asked him to set up his earthly kingdom and appoint himself the judge of all such dilemmas. The religious rulers tried to trap him by asking questions that fell at the intersection of prophecy and deception. Today the contemporary church is embroiled in debates over claims that God is doing a new thing and we must abandon the old ways.

Jesus frustrated everyone who tried to pin him on the horns of such a dilemma. He did not provide formulas for discerning truth from falsehood. Instead he told ambiguous parables. They are ambiguous not because Jesus wanted to escape the responsibility of answering the questions. They are ambiguous because he knew that revealing the answers was less important than exposing the hearts of those who asked the questions. "If anyone has ears to hear, let him hear" (Mk 4:23). A heart still mired in deception will hear distortion, while a heart open to truth will hear truth in the parable.

Jesus said that his sheep recognize their master's voice (Jn 10:4, 27). They do not need others to confirm that they have heard it, because they will not be deceived by false voices (Jn 10:5). The only way to distinguish illumination from deception is to spend more time listening to the master's voice than we spend listening to the voices of others.

UNION: CONTINUING CLOSENESS

What happens after we have seen the light in the illuminative stage? Mountaintop experiences cannot last forever. We have to come down sometime.

I remember as an adolescent going to church camp or spiritual retreats and coming back "high on the love of Jesus." Everyone around us
knows it can't last. We may try to hang on to the mountaintop experience, like Peter who wanted to set up tents for Jesus, Moses and Elijah
on the mount of transfiguration (Mt 17; Mk 9; Lk 9). Eventually, like
the disciples. we have to come back down the mountain.

When Moses came down from the mountain where he met with the
Lord, his face was so radiant that he needed to cover it with a veil so that
the people would not be frightened of him (Ex 34:33). But he kept the
veil on long after coming down from the mountain, to hide the reality
that the radiance eventually faded (2 Cor 3:13).

After illumination comes a time of adjusting to change. We have
been changed, and the changes need to become part of daily life. Tradition names this the *unitive* stage. We have had an intimate encounter with
God, and we remain intimately connected with him. After the awe of
illumination wears off, the closeness which follows is less extreme but
no less welcome. We live in greater harmony with God and with those
around us. The struggle and anguish of purgation are now memories,
and the watershed of illumination becomes a story that we tell. To use a
software metaphor, now we go about the task of living Life 2.0.

We spend most of our lives in the intervals before and after illumination. No one could live on a mountaintop forever. It is exciting up there,
but it is also overwhelming.

Union is the stage we wish could last forever. Union with God
is the condition for which we were created, and the condition from
which sin separates us. The unitive stage is a taste of what heaven
will be like. Union is where we want to live, but in a fallen world
it quickly fades. The place where we once found union becomes the
place of slavery.

Union with God is not a destination; it is a journey. We cannot hold
on to union with God by memorializing the places where we found it.

Good water, if it does not have a continual source of renewal, will become stagnant. In a similar way our spiritual lives, fed by nothing but memories of past intimacy with God, will stagnate.

The Israelites did not finally achieve peace and contentment once they arrived at the Promised Land. Union with God was what they already had in the wilderness, not something they were waiting to acquire. They walked intimately with their God in the wilderness. They had to be sure to continue to walk intimately with God in their new home as well.

Moses knew dependence on God would be more difficult in the land of milk and honey because the people would become complacent (Deut 11). Many movements in the church and elsewhere start in a passion of revival, then gradually stagnate into artificiality. Like Moses' veil, the traditions and customs of the past eventually cover over the fact that the radiance has faded. Rather than seek something new, we keep on with vain repetitions, hoping the original spark might be rekindled.

Stagnation is the surest sign of the need to reenter the wilderness. In my experience spiritual dryness is not usually a result of blatant sin or rebellion. Stagnation is more likely to come when God's pillar of cloud and fire has moved on, and we have not followed it.

Imagine if the Israelites had settled at the rock where God provided water and refused to move on when God moved. When the water dried up, they would have died. Spiritually we dry up and begin to die when we idolize those things, or places or people that God used to refresh us in the desert. We superstitiously return to the same places, wondering why the miracle doesn't happen again.

WHO MOVED?

I disagree with the common Christian saying "If God seems far away, it isn't God who moved." God moves all the time. Often he waits patiently for us just around the bend while we sit down and pout about how he used to be where we are now.

The Christian journey is one of rhythm and movement, not stagnation. God is unchanging in his holiness, but he is not tame and contained. When we begin to think we have God safely figured out, it is time for God to move.

Psalm 137 speaks of God's rhythm, back and forth, reminiscent of the journey in the wilderness. First he makes rivers into a desert to humble his people. Then he turns the desert into gardens where the humbled can live. They become arrogant again and he takes them back to the wilderness. Then he lifts them again out of their misery.

> He turned rivers into a desert,
>> flowing springs into thirsty ground,
> and fruitful land into a salt waste,
>> because of the wickedness of those who lived there.
> He turned the desert into pools of water
>> and the parched ground into flowing springs;
> there he brought the hungry to live,
>> and they founded a city where they could settle.
> They sowed fields and planted vineyards
>> that yielded a fruitful harvest;
> he blessed them, and their numbers greatly increased,
>> and he did not let their herds diminish.
> Then their numbers decreased, and they were humbled
>> by oppression, calamity and sorrow;
> he who pours contempt on nobles
>> made them wander in a trackless waste.
> But he lifted the needy out of their affliction
>> and increased their families like flocks.
> The upright see and rejoice,

but all the wicked shut their mouths.
Whoever is wise, let him heed these things
     and consider the great love of the Lord. (Ps 137:33-43)

The upright see that God is involved in every stage of the journey, even the unpleasant parts. God does not stay put. His loving rhythm will take us to the places where we encounter exactly what we need to grow.

The cycle of the stages of the spiritual way is lifelong. With maturity we do not lose the need to follow after God. What we lose is our stubborn resistance to his movement. Like the Israelites at the end of their wilderness trek, following God becomes second nature to the spiritually mature person.

I like to imagine what it was like for the Israelites who stood at the brink of the Jordan River ready to enter the Promised Land. I think that many of them, especially the young ones, found the prospect rather frightening. Never mind the fact that there were wicked nations to be conquered. I think the idea of settling down in one place was frightening as well. After a lifetime of traveling everywhere with one's clan, now people would spread out and inhabit different areas. Instead of gathering manna from heaven every morning, they would have to raise and harvest their food. To the Israelite nomads, life in one place probably sounded overwhelming.

God does not want us to follow him only when our lives literally depend on it. He wants us to follow him in the good times too. He wants us to be willing to drop everything we have built up with our own hands and take off with him into the wilderness.

RADICAL READINESS

A would-be disciple asked Jesus if he could follow him after he first went to bury his father. Jesus answered him, "Follow me, and let the dead bury their own dead" (Mt 8:22). Another wanted to follow Jesus after he went to say goodbye to his family. Jesus answered him, "No one who puts his hand to the plow and looks back is fit for service in the kingdom of God" (Lk 9:62). These are hard sayings. Jesus wants a radical readiness to follow him. When we see God moving, nothing should hinder us from following after him

The spiritual life will never be boring. The cycle of purgation, illumination and union will keep repeating all of our days. The nature of the cycle will change as we mature, but the need to have times in the wilderness of purgation will never stop.

I like to think of the stages of our spiritual life paralleling the three characters in Jesus' parable of the lost son (Lk 15:11-31).

The younger son, the one we call the prodigal, shows the spiritually immature qualities of pride and resistance to God's direction. In the end it is his mercenary motives, not his virtuous character, which brings him back to the father. He is not being noble when he says to himself, "How many of my father's hired men have food to spare, and here I am starving to death!" (Lk 15:17). Like the Israelites at the beginning of their pilgrimage, the younger son has little patience for discomfort and inconvenience. He wallows in the purgative stage before he finally submits to having his eyes opened to the reality of his father's loving care.

The older brother illustrates a more mature but still imperfect image of his father. His obedience is not as fickle or mercenary as his brother's. It is the obedience of one who follows the rules. Like many in the church, he does what is right and has always been right. He doesn't rock the boat, and he expects to be his father's favorite because of it. He resents the attention lavished on his disrespectful, immature brother. When the father runs out of the city to greet the brother and kills the fatted calf to feast in honor of the brother's return, the older son does not follow after the father. Instead he grows angry that the father is disrupting the routine that has always worked so well. He does not like this new side of his father.

Of the three characters in the parable, the father shows us the goal for our obedience. His desire is only to be with both of his sons. While he enjoys the presence of the older son, he continually watches and waits for his younger son. He lives every day ready to drop everything, hitch up his robes and run out to embrace the returning prodigal. The father's loves are in the proper order. Society's rules and expectations do not concern him, especially when they conflict with what he knows to be most important. He does not place anything, including his own reputation, ahead of his love for his sons. Union, or in this case reunion, is foremost on the father's mind.

A SPIRITUAL SPIRAL

The nature of the way of spiritual formation changes as we mature. At the beginning we are more resistant and defensive against God's leading. We want to control our own way. We do not want to follow every time God decides it is time to move. We spend more time in the purgative stage, resisting God's desire to strip away our addictions and illusions. Our periods of union with God are briefer as well because our pride leads us to quickly take credit for the good things in our lives and forget God's hand in providing them.

As we mature, we are less resistant to God. We are more able to make use of the purgative stage once we arrive in the wilderness. We hold on to the lessons longer and are not as quick to stagnate. Like the older brother in Jesus' parable, we are reliable, obedient children, even if we are not wholly attentive to the Father's will.

With maturity, the spiritual way becomes a comfortable well-traveled path. We do not resist the purgative stage. We willingly enter it when God calls us there, and we do not resist its lessons. We linger, too, in the unitive stage. The humbled soul is less eager to take control away from God. The mature believer has consistently found God's way to be so much better than stagnating into self-determination.

And so we cycle in our spiritual journey. We enter the wilderness either willingly or by surprise. Willing purgation is found in spiritual disciplines we practice either at penitent times such as Lent or in our daily spiritual life. Living brings along its own wilderness through many kinds of loss and trial. In those times we are purified as in a crucible. Our sin is brought to the surface so that it may be stripped away. Our eyes are opened in illumination as we see God's hand in the purging. We incarnate these changes into a deeper relationship with God. Finally we settle back into some old or new patterns of sin and separation from God, and the whole cycle must be repeated.

Our signature sins come to play in the cycle because they are usually involved in the repetition. They creep back in after they have been cast out. They whisper in our ears, trying to persuade us that we don't really want to live without them. They come back in disguised form.

Spiritual maturity means coming around to the same struggle but from a better vantage point. One of the advantages of a long-term relationship in spiritual direction is that others can see more clearly than we can see how much we have matured. They can reassure us that although our sins may be the same, our cyclical journey is moving ever upward.

TAMING YOUR WAYWARD HEART

- What are the landmarks that you keep encountering on your own journey around the mountain?

- Where are you in the cycle of purgation, illumination, union and stagnation?

    Where do you need to head next?

- In your journal, name the times of most powerful purgation in your life. What changed as a result of those experiences, though you might not of have seen it at the time?

- Have you experienced a "dark night" as described by John of the Cross?

   When God seemed far away, what comforted you most?

   What do you need to remember the next time that a spiritual dry spell comes?

- When you have reached a time of spiritual stagnation, what keeps you from going back into the wilderness to refresh your experience of God?

12

Restoring Spiritual Balance

JESUS DID NOT TAKE A ONE-SIZE-FITS-ALL APPROACH TO SIN. He discerned the heart of each person and named the sin which held the hearer in its clutches like the spider hidden at the center of the web. Time after time Jesus' gift of discernment cut to the heart of the matter. He carefully tailored his responses to the readiness and openness of the person to whom he was speaking.

When Jesus confronted the Pharisees, he was blunt and even insulting. Not only was their blindness to the truth deeply engrained in their own rotten, tomblike souls, but by their very self-righteousness they kept others from knowing God's love and grace. At other times Jesus was as gentle and precise as a spiritual surgeon.

When a woman was caught in adultery and brought by the Pharisees to be stoned, Jesus turned the focus onto their sin instead (Jn 8:1-11). He commanded that whoever among them was without sin should throw the first stone. The tables were neatly turned. I read or heard this Scripture passage many times before I finally noticed what happened next. "At this, those who heard began to go away one at a time, *the older ones first*" (Jn 8:9, emphasis added). Why the older ones first? The answer is simple. While no one is immune from the temptation to pride and self-righteousness, they afflict the young more than the old.

How did Jesus' confrontation of the woman's adultery compare with his confrontation of the Pharisees' whitewashed tombs? After noting that no one else had stayed to condemn her and neither would he, Jesus simply stated that she should go and leave her life of sin.

To those whose hearts were hardened, Jesus' confrontations had the gentleness of a sledgehammer. To those who had ears to hear, as the woman apparently had, his reprimands were so gentle that they hardly seemed like confrontations at all.

Sin and sinners come in many varieties. The confrontation of sin needs to be tailored to the sinner. The spiritual life will take different forms depending on each person's battles and victories.

DIFFERENT STREAMS

When I lead a retreat or teach a workshop on spiritual formation, I often begin by displaying a small poster. The illustrator has depicted the stream of Christian church history graphically as a sort of river. On the left side is a cross. From the cross, the church flows out like a river growing ever wider to the present day. At key dates along the timeline, the stream divides into different colors and currents within the larger stream.

On the river diagram there is a division at the time of the split between the Eastern Orthodox and Roman Catholic churches and another at the Protestant Reformation. In addition to the major divisions there are many smaller ones. Splits and schisms are illustrated by different shades of the parent color. The overall effect is quite striking.

Everyone who looks at the diagram of church history immediately sets to work finding the small or large current of his or her personal tradition within the broader river of the church. After everyone looks at the diagram for a moment, I ask people to share their initial reactions. The first reaction is usually something like, "There are so many divisions and fights within the church. It's too bad we can't all get along."

The second reaction is usually something like, "Wow! It's great to see all the denominations laid out in one stream. There is a place for everyone in the church."

The two reactions to the river illustration are opposite sides of the same coin. People killed each other over some of the disagreements on the poster. Denominations continue to divide people today. On the other hand, the illustration reveals Christians' passion to protect and defend the truth. Each division came because some group believed that the church was neglecting some aspect of God's truth.

The passion to protect neglected truths has resulted in diverse streams of the church with traditions and experience that can benefit the whole. The ambivalent, two-sided coin is the church that we all love and hate.

God's truth is simply too big for us to grasp. We can view only a few facets of it at a time. While we are looking at one facet, we cannot see the facets on the other side that a brother or sister in Christ can see. Our vision is limited whether we are gazing at theological tenets, musical taste or communion beverage. As a result of the Fall, we place the greatest importance on the parts of God's truth which we can see, and we devalue the parts which are out of our range of vision.

It is easy to get caught up in the differentness of Christian diversity and lose sight of its richness. This is why I have such respect for the Renovaré model of spiritual formation. Richard Foster's book *Streams of Living Water: Celebrating the Great Traditions of Christian Faith* presents six streams of spirituality illustrated in Jesus' life and in the life of the church. Foster and his team look at the different faces of Christian spirituality and see not division but depth. They say that the different streams of the church reflect different aspects of Christ's nature as evidenced in the incarnation. Each different tradition of the church has kept alive something which should not be lost. Each tradition has gifts which will help bring about change in our character. Each has unique weapons to contribute to our battle with sin.

CONTEMPLATIVE: QUIET LISTENING

The contemplative tradition of Christianity is modeled after Jesus' prayer life and teachings on intimacy with God. Those drawn to the contemplative stream of spirituality hunger for deeper union with God above all else. They seek to withdraw and be alone as Jesus retreated from the crowds to be with his Father. Within many denominations there have been those who sought the contemplative life of quiet prayer. The Quaker movement is known for an emphasis on contemplation. Those with a contemplative temperament long to get away from busyness and superficiality and to be alone with God.

The contemplative tradition helps us quiet ourselves enough to hear God's voice. We cannot hear the Holy Spirit call us to transformation if we continually distract ourselves. Silence and solitude open our hearts so that the Spirit can illuminate the dark corners. This is, of course, why many people are also frightened of contemplation.

HOLINESS: STRIVING AND SEEKING

The holiness tradition is modeled after Jesus' battle with Satan in the desert and his teaching about the importance of a pure heart. The holiness tradition emphasizes striving against sin and seeking after virtue. John Wesley taught his followers to emphasize this stream of spirituality. The Methodist, Nazarene and Salvation Army denominations are examples from this stream. The holiness tradition offers some of the best writings for believers who seek to overcome sin. With its call to righteousness, the holiness tradition sets many pilgrims on the road toward Christlikeness.

CHARISMATIC: THE POWER OF THE SPIRIT

The charismatic tradition is modeled after Jesus' ministry and empowerment by the Spirit. Jesus emphasized healing, wisdom and strength from the Comforter. Pentecostal churches follow in this tradition, as do charismatic believers in every denomination. This tradition values the present power of the Holy Spirit to act in the world in miraculous ways. Too many Christians neglect the gifts of the charismatic tradition. Its emphasis on the power of the Spirit to transform us into Christ's image is especially needed as we pray for God's transformation of our signature sins into their corresponding virtues.

SOCIAL JUSTICE: BEYOND OUR OWN INTEREST

The social justice tradition is modeled after Jesus' ministry to the sick and the needy and his teaching about compassion and care for our neighbors. Believers in this tradition seek to bring aid to those who are suffering. They advocate for the powerless and show Christ's love through acts of service. The Anabaptist tradition, particularly the Mennonites, follows in this stream with their powerful witness of uniting as one community to stand against a materialistic and self-centered world. Many mainline denominations also emphasize this expression of Christian spirituality. The social justice tradition has much to offer to take us beyond our own self-interest and to teach us about living in community.

EVANGELICAL: PROCLAIMING GOOD NEWS

The evangelical tradition is modeled after Jesus' proclamation of the good news of the kingdom of heaven and his teaching on the centrality of the Scriptures. The missionary movements around the world are in this stream of Christian spirituality. Most Baptists and many independent churches fit squarely in this tradition. The study of Scripture as a means of knowing God is foundational to the evangelical stream. Too many people count themselves Christians and participate in Christian community but neglect the study of God's Word. The evangelical tradition holds up Scripture as the primary means for conviction of sin and understanding the promise of forgiveness and transformation.

Incarnational: Christ with Us

The incarnational tradition was the final category added to the Renovaré streams. Jesus' integration of the sacred and the secular, faith and work, physical and spiritual in his practice and in his teaching inspires this tradition. The incarnational tradition opposes all forms of gnosticism. This category is not exemplified by any single denomination. Those who emphasize the importance of living out one's faith in day-to-day life follow in this stream. Traditions which emphasize symbolism and liturgy also characterize this stream. Iconography, stained glass windows, imposition of ashes, anointing with oil, baptizing with water and burning of incense all follow in the tradition of the priests and artisans of the Old Testament temple and in the incarnational tradition. This tradition helps to keep us mindful that spiritual formation results in and is a result of active integration of Christ into our daily lives.

The six streams of Christian spirituality are not meant to be mutually exclusive. Like the temperaments discussed in earlier chapters, the streams represent different areas of strength in the spiritual life.

Spokes in a Wheel

In an exercise in *A Spiritual Formation Workbook* the reader is encouraged to imagine each of the six streams as a spoke in a wheel. Are some of the spokes shorter than others, causing one's wheel to bump? We are encouraged to seek a balanced spirituality, one strong in all six of the streams.

All good things can be taken to an extreme. Each of the six traditions has examples of excess. Those who emphasize the contemplative tradition to the exclusion of all others may forget to take action and make their faith practical. Excesses in the holiness tradition have historically caused the church to become bogged down in legalism. The charismatic movement has tended toward excesses of emotionality and valuing certain charisms over others. The social justice tradition can end in the extreme of caring for people's physical needs and forgetting to feed their souls. The evangelical tradition has sometimes cared more about saving souls than about filling stomachs, and it can turn love of Scripture into bibliolatry. The incarnational tradition can place beauty, symbolism and ceremony above the message and can forget that the integration of faith and daily life is not more important than faith itself.

Every believer feels more at home in one or more of these streams than in others. If we have grown up in the church, we probably prefer the stream from which we came, simply because it feels right to us. Those who didn't grow up in any one Christian tradition may prefer the tradition through which they entered the faith.

Having grown up in the evangelical stream, I know the language of that stream very well. I know the culture, the hymns, the theological debates and the prejudices. I even know the heroes and the villains.

I recently found a CD by an artist who recorded many of the old gospel hymns he sang as a child. As a boy I sang the same songs in church. None of those songs is in the hymnbook of my current church, and I haven't sung most of them in over twenty years. As I listened I still remembered most of the verses, many of them based on Scripture. I find that Scripture often comes to mind at those times when I need it most. It usually comes to mind in the King James Version that I memorized in Sunday school. I am thankful for God's Word that I hid in my heart long ago, where it simultaneously challenges and comforts me. I continue to be fed by my evangelical roots and never want to take those roots for granted.

On the other hand I am not very familiar with the culture of the charismatic stream. People in my tradition were frightened of the charismatic tradition. I heard sermons preached against speaking in tongues. They were scary stories meant to keep us from wandering over in that direction. My roots are shallow in the riches which the charismatic stream has to offer.

There is nothing wrong with cherishing favorite hymns, familiar liturgies and a style of worship with which we are comfortable. The danger arises when we idolize our preferences and demand that others do the same. We stagnate spiritually when we expect all spiritual nourishment to come from one stream. We miss the balance provided by the other traditions.

AWAKENING TO PRAYER

I remember the burst of exciting growth in my spiritual life when I discovered, in young adulthood, the contemplative stream. Growing up in the evangelical stream I was taught to have regular devotions consisting of Bible study and discursive prayer structured around a list of petitions that I should regularly bring to God. I confess that this type of time with God was always dry and difficult for me. I had been taught that prayer is hard work. It was a discipline one engaged in whether it was enjoyable or not.

When I began to read the classic contemplative writings, something awoke in me that had been sleeping for a long time. As a child on our Montana farm I spent many hours out on the prairie walking and talking with my friend Jesus. As I grew up in the evangelical church, I was taught that prayer is structured, it is organized, it is scheduled and it is hard work. I abandoned my times of hanging out with Jesus as only childish imaginings.

When I began to read John of the Cross, Henri Nouwen, and the sayings of the desert fathers and mothers, I felt more at home than I had ever felt before. Though the culture and history of many of the writings in contemplative spirituality were unfamiliar to me, my temperament had found the place where it belonged. I began to relish the thought of getting up early in the morning for contemplative silent prayer. I spent hours in worshipful silence, freed from the guilt of not having made it through my shopping list of prayer requests. I felt I had discovered a secret: that God actually liked to *be* with me, not just hear all my requests and problems.

In a similar way, when I began attending a liturgical church I was wonderfully overwhelmed by the richness of the incarnational tradition. The symbolism and ceremony of the liturgy spoke to my soul. Communion took on powerful new meaning for me. It was months before I went forward to receive the sacrament with dry eyes. The rhythm of the church year spoke to my heart about the story of Jesus' life in ways that only hearing about it had never accomplished. I felt more a part of the cloud of witnesses through all the centuries because of a shared liturgical tradition.

Finding the tradition which satisfied my spiritual temperament also transformed my struggle against sin. It is difficult to seek holiness when we are spiritually undernourished. When I did not enjoy time with God, I had little motivation (other than guilt) to become more holy. When I began to know God more intimately through times of contemplative prayer, I longed to please him and to be transformed into the likeness of his Son.

I did not stop appreciating my evangelical heritage. My roots there are deep and I continue to draw strength from them. I depend daily on God's Word that I hid in my heart decades ago, when I memorized Scripture in Sunday school. I am thankful for my clear understanding of theology and doctrine that comes from my evangelical roots. Still my spiritual life needed the refreshment of alternative streams of Christian spirituality.

UNFAMILIAR STREAMS

While some Christian streams feel like home, others feel foreign and even frightening. Take my resistance to the charismatic tradition. Although I wish it were not true, I am uncomfortable with charismatic worship. In my memory I still hear all those sermons about the danger of getting caught up in the emotionalism of charismania. I was taught that the charisms of the spirit were only for the age immediately following Jesus' ascension and not for today—something I no longer believe. Some charismatic Christians I knew did little to reassure me since they exhibited the unhealthy extremes that I feared.

Even if I had not been taught to fear the charismatic stream, my temperament would have led me away from it. I am not an openly emotional person. I like things to be calm and reasonable. I like to feel in control. My temperament put me right at home in the evangelical stream and even in the contemplative and incarnational streams when I discovered them. By contrast the charismatic stream pushes me out of my comfort zone. I don't trust what I can't explain. I especially do not like strong emotions that come on a person unbidden. Yet all those things I fear are characteristic of the Holy Spirit.

I used to get away with the rationalization that the charismatic tradition is immature and dangerous; therefore I didn't have to deal with those aspects of God that made me uncomfortable. The God of my upbringing is orderly and predictable. He certainly wouldn't make people start spouting other languages or crying, laughing or shaking for no reason whatsoever. I am thankful that God has gently but persistently worn away my defenses against his character as expressed in the charismatic stream.

God's wooing toward the more emotional aspects of spirituality began when he playfully matched me up with the perfect freshman roommate at Wheaton College. I—a stoic fundamentalist farm boy from Montana—roomed with a charismatic Italian Catholic from New Jersey.

What a year! As the two of us struggled to understand each other, we could not escape our common faith. No matter how many ways we were different, we were first and foremost brothers in Christ. I wanted to dismiss my roommate and by extension dismiss his faith as well. As we grew to care for each other, I found that his faith had a passion and vitality that I admired and longed for.

The charismatic stream continues to stretch me as I learn to trust the power and presence of the Holy Spirit. I have learned from those gifted in this stream how little I expect of God. I pray, but I don't really think God will do anything surprising. I want to have a bolder faith. I want to be open to a deeper experience of God's love. Combating my signature sins requires me to venture more and more into the charismatic stream.

Sin thrives in a spiritually unbalanced life, and the other streams of Christianity now serve to make me more balanced as a believer. Jesus was the only person who ever exhibited perfect spiritual balance. All the rest of us must work at it.

Balance is a long-term goal. I cannot expect to achieve it today or even this month or this year. I need to set my sights on becoming more like Christ over a long journey. But if I am already stronger in some areas than in others, what is the point of continuing to put all my time and attention into those streams? I need to be stretched. I need to learn from those who are gifted in the areas where I am not.

At different times the Holy Spirit has led me into unfamiliar waters as I needed their healing influence. When I first discovered the contemplative tradition, I immersed myself in it. When I was ill for several months from a bad reaction to a medication, I had to depend heavily on others' prayers for healing, and I found myself immersed in the gifts of the charismatic tradition. When I first attended a liturgical church after decades in traditional evangelical churches, I was profoundly affected by the different style of worship and immersed myself in that tradition.

God often sees fit to call us out of comfortable places and into places that will stretch us. Sometimes we don't recognize that the place where we are has become a prison or a place of slavery. Our unwillingness to accept change or loss keeps us from moving into the new place that God has prepared for us.

WILDERNESS WAGON TRAIN

My brother is part of a group that re-creates the pioneer wagon trains of the old West. For more than thirty years they have gathered every fall to travel across the prairie for several days in wagons and on horseback. The route is different every year. Once I participated in a wagon train in my hometown of Malta, Montana. I have never been to the deserts of the Middle East, but when I read about the Israelites leaving Egypt or about Jesus going out to be tempted in the wilderness, I imagine being on the prairie of Montana and the Dakotas.

A wagon train provides the best metaphor I know for the forty-year wilderness trek of the Israelites and for life's spiritual journey. God took his people out of the slavery of Egypt and into the Promised Land. Along the way he gave them the Law and taught them who they were to become. God led the people through places where their experiences developed their relationship with him. He led them across the sea. He fed them with quail and manna. He gave them water from rocks. He led them with a pillar of fire and cloud. Every part of their journey with God carried a lesson.

The wilderness journey took forty years. I can imagine the Israelites grumbling like bored children, "Are we there yet?" We might assume that God took an inordinately long time to bring his people to their new home or that he was punishing them for forty years. In the book of Deuteronomy, Moses told a different story. He recalled how God intimately traveled with his people in the wilderness. They learned to depend on God for everything from protection and food to the direction of their travel. The journey was far more important than the destination. If God had only intended for them to reach Canaan, the trip would have been much shorter.

One summer my wife and I traveled with our newly adolescent son to Montana to see my family. Because of commitments back home we were able to stay there for only two days. The schedule meant that we would travel 2,500 miles, four days of driving, for two days with my family. Although some people thought it was odd, we didn't hesitate to do it. Four days of uninterrupted family time were as precious as gold. We talked and laughed and listened to recorded books. We had to make decisions and solve problems together. We also got on each other's nerves and argued without being able to retreat to our separate rooms or numb ourselves with the television. I wouldn't trade those four days in the car for anything.

I wonder if God felt like that in the wilderness with his children. During their travels their attention was on him. They had to follow him or they would get lost. They had to learn to trust his goodness. They had to face their sinfulness. Maybe he regretted having to let them settle down when they finally arrived at the Promised Land. Moses seems to have regretted the end of the journey. In his sermon to the people of Israel he didn't speak of the forty-year pilgrimage as a difficult or wasted time. He spoke of it quite fondly. He talked about the remarkable and wonderful provision of the Lord. He warned them of the danger of settling into the new country after the intimacy they had enjoyed with the Father in the wilderness. Sin would begin to take over when they lost their intimate walk with God.

Except for a few whom God gave special dispensation to see the Promised Land, all the people Moses addressed in Deuteronomy had been born in the wilderness. One by one the people who had known slavery and idolatry had died off. God basically started from scratch with his people in the Promised Land. The new people of Israel did not know anything except traveling intimately with God. They had grown up following the pillar of cloud and fire, depending wholly on God for every need.

The pilgrimage transforms the pilgrim. Every person is on a pilgrimage toward the object of his or her devotion. We are formed into the likeness of that to which we have attached our hearts. In the final chapter we will look at the importance of being intentional and thoughtful about our spiritual journeys.

6

TAMING YOUR WAYWARD HEART

- Which of the six spiritual streams are you most familiar with?

    Were you raised in that tradition?

    Why is it most familiar?

- Are any of the six streams frightening or uncomfortable to you?

    What experiences or messages have led to your resistance?

- Which stream is most comforting to you?

    What practices or aspects of that stream do you miss if you are away from it for a while?

- In which stream is God calling you to be spiritually stretched?

    How can you seek out an introduction to and greater appreciation for that stream?

- What does a balanced spiritual life look like for you?

13

Becoming Who We Are in Christ

YEARS AGO I TRAVELED TO INDIA to teach with some students and colleagues. Many things about the journey transformed my understanding of myself, of the world and of God.

After I returned from India I had a dream. In the dream I was in a room. I recognized this room as "my" room, the room of my life, although it did not mirror any actual room in any place I have ever lived. In the dream I gradually became aware that the walls of my room were not walls at all but were sheets of gauze hanging where I had always believed the walls should be. I refocused my eyes and could see through the gauze wall. Outside were innumerable people in every direction as far as I could see.

My dream simultaneously thrilled and terrified me. Two words describe my reaction: *disillusionment* and *enlightenment*.

In one sense disillusionment and enlightenment both mean seeing something in a new way. In another sense they are opposites. Disillusionment usually refers to a painful experience; comfortable illusions are stripped away. Enlightenment usually refers to exciting insight; I understand something more clearly than before.

My dream, which summarized my trip to India, represented the unsettling removal of illusions. My world could never again be small and predictable. The dream also reflected bright new understanding. My world would now be larger and more exciting. My heart had been stretched in its capacity to love a bigger world.

HEARTS ON PILGRIMAGE

Not only were my eyes opened to see a bigger world out there; I also saw myself and my old world with new eyes. When I tried to fit back into the rhythm of my old life, aspects which had seemed normal began to chafe at me. I saw the blatant materialism and consumerism around me with greater distaste. I understood with increased urgency the injustice of a tiny percentage of the world's population hoarding so many of the world's resources. I had a greater sense that I was one individual in a world of billions. I saw not only the sins of the world but my own participation in sin. I felt convicted to take my proper place in relation to God and my fellow human beings.

When I return from a trip like the one to India, I am exhausted and relieved to be home. I do not want to turn around and immediately leave on another expedition. It isn't too long, however, before I start itching to travel again. I both long to travel and dread it a little. I know the journey will change me. For a time I will step out of my normal life and see it from the outside. The prospect scares me and invigorates me.

The psalmist wrote, "Blessed are those whose strength is in you, / who have set their hearts on pilgrimage" (Ps 84:5). A pilgrimage is a trip, usually to a holy site, meant to demonstrate the pilgrim's devotion to something larger than himself or herself. A heart set on pilgrimage does not settle for the comfortable and ordinary.

Literature and history offer many stories of those who pursue great quests. Ulysses, Columbus, King Arthur, Magellan, Bilbo Baggins, Lewis and Clark, Prince Caspian, Sir Edmund Hillary, Christian (in *The Pilgrim's Progress*), Neil Armstrong, Huckleberry Finn and the voyagers on the *Mayflower* conjure up images of epic ventures. All of them pursued the journey rather than staying comfortable.

SEEN FROM THE ROAD

Where I grew up in rural Montana, distance is relative. We had to drive two hundred miles to get to a city large enough for a major airport. It was not unusual to drive ninety miles or more to go shopping or see a medical specialist. Trips to visit relatives in other states required several days in the car.

In my mid-twenties I flew for the first time on a trip to California. During my entire stay in California I was aware of a vague feeling of having somehow cheated. I shouldn't be able to be someplace so far away within a matter of hours. California should represent at least three days of driving, yet there I was on the same morning I departed.

Now I am accustomed to the convenience of flying and I take it for granted, but I still like long road trips. I feel that I know a place best if I can experience it in its context. I think of cities I have flown in and out for conferences. Most of those cities remain a mystery to me since I experienced them only in the form of an airport and a hotel.

Cities to which I travel by car or train feel more familiar. I can visualize them in the context of the greater geography. I remember the journey to get there, whether alone or with others. I remember the excitement and sense of exploration as I finally arrived at my destination. I don't always have time for road trips and I am thankful that air travel is available. When I travel by air, however, I remember mostly the purpose of my visit, not my journey to get there.

This book has been about the spiritual journey to confront our signature sins and become more like Christ. Like a quest or a pilgrimage to a holy site, the spiritual life is about more than the destination. We are changed by our experiences along the way. In the journey we make choices, overcome obstacles, evaluate our lives and alter our priorities. Most important, on our spiritual journeys we learn to depend on God.

While some of my most enjoyable trips involved spontaneous route changes, I try to begin every trip with a plan. I have an intended route, a definite direction, a specific destination, places where I expect to stop and rest, an estimated time of arrival, an idea of how long I will stay, and target dates for leaving and for arriving back home. I have never set out on a journey without pinning down at least some of those details.

How odd it is that most people approach the spiritual journey with far less preparation than they would approach a prospective cross-country road trip. They plan their careers, the size of their family and their retirement, but they give little or no thought to *who* they want to become spiritually. They let their souls be formed by the random course of life, taking no thought to exercise influence over the process.

If the person with an unplanned spiritual life comes into contact with others whose spiritual lives are relatively mature, the person may grow in a healthy direction. I have known people who are morally good despite their lack of attention to their own spiritual growth. Generally I find that they are only one or two generations removed from someone who *did* pay attention to sin and righteousness. The children and grandchildren of righteous people carry on fairly well with the momentum left over from previous godly generations, even if they do not generate much momentum of their own. The next generation after the stragglers bears evidence of the lack of spiritual direction. If they fall under ungodly influences and neglect to correct their course, their souls will wither and grow away from God.

DEVELOPING DEPTH

Just as most people think they have above average intelligence, I suspect that most people feel they are deep. Who wants to admit to being shallow? Superficiality prefers the simple explanations of "reality lite." A spiritually deep person must prefer painful, inconvenient reality over comfortable illusion.

When my son was born, I found myself in a dilemma. As a father I wanted to protect my child from all sadness, pain and loss. At the same time I knew he could reach spiritual maturity and depth only through difficult experiences. How could I want both depth and protection for him at the same time? I discovered, as every parent discovers, that life provides more than enough unavoidable pain. Even the best parent cannot protect a child from every hurt. My job became to help my son grapple with pain and make meaning from it in the best way possible. I could only try to keep his pain from being more than his soul could bear at each stage of his development.

Pain comes inevitably in a fallen, sinful world. God our Father desires to help us find the right path through the unique form of suffering that each of us will encounter. Fortunately our God wastes nothing. God can transform every hurt into depth of character.

We cannot produce our own spiritual depth; it comes only with God's help. We do have the power to try to resist the work of God's hand in our lives. Our desire should be to participate willingly in what God is doing in our souls. The quickest roadmap to the place where God is working is through the painful wounds that God desires to heal.

During the first few months after my son's birth I went through a time of anger and frustration with God. I demanded promises and guarantees. I wanted to say to God, "When it comes to my child, I want a contract that says nothing really bad will ever happen to him." Like the prodigal's older brother, my attitude toward my Father was "Look, I've been faithful all my life. Shouldn't I get special consideration?" For a while I even kept my distance from God because I wanted to sort out my feelings about the terms of our relationship. I had no doubt that God existed; that was the easy part. My suspicion, as I have noted in previous chapters, was that God is not good. This time of pain and growth revealed my signature sin of pride. I wanted special status with God.

As always, God was patient with me during this time. I felt no guilt or shame about my anger, and I still don't. Mine was every soul's struggle with the question of theodicy: how do we reconcile the experience of evil with the goodness of God?

I vividly remember the night my spiritual fever broke. It was on Good Friday. I was in church, participating distractedly throughout the Good Friday service. A rude cross had been placed at the front of the sanctuary, and during the service congregants could go up to the altar to pray and meditate on the cross. When my turn came I dutifully went forward to kneel. As I knelt there, God's voice spoke in my heart so clearly that it startled me. It was as if God said, "I won't change the terms of the relationship. I won't promise to insulate your son or anyone else's child from the evils of the world. But neither did I take the cup from my Son when the evils of the world came upon him. This was his cross." The word was hard to hear. I didn't like to hear that I could have no promises; I still don't like it. But at least I could no longer argue that it wasn't fair.

CHOOSE YOUR FUTURE

Pilgrims follow the Way wherever it goes. If my eyes are on Christ, no obstacle will distract me from him. If life forces me to take detours, I will find my way back on track as long as I keep my eyes on my destination.

I occasionally engage in a contemplative exercise that helps me stay focused on the destination. I meditate on myself as an old man. I imagine myself near the end of my life. How will I interact with people? What will be important to me? What things which seem important now will have fallen by the wayside? What will I regret? What will I be known for?

A similar exercise involves writing your own eulogy. What would you want said about you at your funeral? How would you like to be remembered?

Such exercises are important because when I choose that person in the future that I would like to become, I have defined a route. Whatever life brings between now and then, I want to make sure I don't lose my bearings and become someone else, someone I don't like, someone who looks nothing like Jesus. If I imagine myself as a kind and gentle old man, but now I am harsh and critical, I need to make sure that the pilgrimage of my life brings about a change in my soul. If I want to be known for my strong faith, I must strengthen my faith now.

Sad to say, we can make colossal mistakes in our choice of who we want to become, especially when our goal is not consistent with Christ's call to us. Many people set their sights on becoming wealthy and successful, only to arrive there and discover that they don't like or respect themselves, and neither does anyone else.

I once led a group in a meditative exercise in which we imagined ourselves as old men or old women. I encouraged each person to mentally walk up to the old self and see what he or she had to say. I also wanted to enter into the exercise, so I closed my eyes and began.

As soon as I closed my eyes, I saw in my imagination myself as an old man sitting in a chair. My old self stood up and quickly walked over to my young self. With urgency in his voice he said, "It's only a little while!" I was stunned back into present reality. Those words, which I believe were spoken by the Holy Spirit, have become a frequent object of my meditation. They speak as deep unto deep.

The words "It's only a little while" have sunk into my soul in two different ways. First, I have spent much of my life worrying about terrible things that might happen to me or to those I love. Will I be able to cope? Will it destroy me? When I meditate on the words "It's only a little while," I realize that with God's always-sufficient grace I will have exactly what I need in order to endure. Nothing that comes can separate me from the love of God. It is only a little while until I will be at home with Jesus.

The second way the words spoke to me was as a wake-up call. "It's only a little while!" I can't put off becoming the man I want to be. While I chase after trivial things, my soul becomes trivial. When my eyes are on shallow and shortsighted objectives, I wander in directions that do nothing to make me into the man God created me to be. When I ignore my signature sins, I waste long periods of time in which God could be transforming me. When I turn my eyes back to Christ, my present circumstance become part of my pilgrimage.

At the front of the sanctuary where I worship is a large wooden Jerusalem cross on a white wall. I sometimes stare at it and then close my eyes. When my eyes are closed the after-image, burned on my retina, is of a white cross on a dark background. I can see it for several seconds before it starts to fade. Within a minute or so the image completely disappears unless I open my eyes and stare at the cross again.

For a while in my spiritual journey I can get by on the memory of where I was going. Before long the image will fade as my eyes are turned away. Echoing Hebrews 12:2, the old hymn reminds us:

> Turn your eyes upon Jesus,
> Look full in His wonderful face;
> And the things of earth will grow strangely dim
> In the light of His glory and grace.

We are pilgrims in a strange land. We are not supposed to settle down here. When we take our eyes off the city on the horizon, Christ's city, we become lost or we settle short of our goal. When we keep the image fresh in our eyes, God gives us the strength to keep on moving.

A SPIRITUAL RULER

While God's Word is a complete and perfect guidebook for our pilgrimage, it is helpful to have a concise summary of its principles for reference along the way. Some traditions have developed a Spiritual Rule or Rule of Life for just that purpose. The Rule is a set of guidelines for daily living.

Postmodern Westerners resist the authoritative sound of the word *rule*. We don't like the idea of any authority outside ourselves. We know how rules can degenerate into meaningless legalism. A Rule of Life, however, is not a list of petty directives; it is more like a carpenter's ruler. We use a ruler to measure accurately so the pieces of the final project fit together. A measuring tape on a child's wall allows for marks which document the child's physical progress toward becoming an adult. A spiritual rule of life enables us to observe our progress as the soul becomes more like Christ.

The most well-known Christian Rule came from St. Benedict of Nursia, the founder of the Benedictine spiritual order. His Rule was intended for practical application. Its purpose was to create order so the people of a community could live in greater harmony. He called it a simple way for beginners to live the teaching of the Scriptures. Many people have successfully adapted the Benedictine rule for ordering one's private life in ways similar to how Benedictine monks order their corporate life.

Other religious orders have developed their own rules for their own order. Some groups and individuals have created guidelines but called them something besides a Rule, for example a personal mission statement or a spiritual action plan. What all have in common is the intention of drawing the follower toward the image of Christ. There are helpful resources for understanding the tradition of the Rule of Life and developing a Rule of one's own. Let me suggest several guidelines for a personal Rule of Life based on the themes I have presented so far.

A Rule should seek balance in the historic streams of Christian spirituality we explored in the previous chapter. Because I grew up in the evangelical tradition, I value the depth of understanding of Scripture and theology which I gained there. I hope I will always continue to grow in my understanding of God's Word. My own deepest roots will continually feed my soul; but I want my Rule of Life to also challenge me to grow where my roots are shallow.

Jesus' compassionate ministry to those poor in spirit and his desire for his followers to believe in the power that comes from trusting in the Holy Spirit are a constant challenge for me. If I want to develop a greater balance in my spiritual life, I need to learn from other branches of the Christian stream such as the charismatic and social justice traditions.

A spiritual Rule of Life should seek balance over the long term. Progress in the less familiar streams should be measured in years and decades, not weeks or even months.

Years ago when I first developed a personal Rule for my spiritual formation, I included the following two rules to stretch me toward greater balance and confront my signature sins.

I will strive to awaken my longing for intimacy with God rather than settling for simple obedience.

I will be more courageous in looking for answers to prayer.

Seven years after I first wrote those words, I can see slow growth in both areas. When I imagine myself forty years from now I see a man who prays boldly, expecting to see God's hand at work, and who rests always in the comfort of God's tangible presence. Those are qualities that I see in my Lord Jesus, and I want him to bring those qualities to fruition in me as well.

AVOIDING RUTS

Like all good stories, our lives have chapters. As the old saying goes, change is the only constant. As we seek to deepen our spiritual roots we will sometimes have to leave the comfort of the familiar and seek out what new things God wants to do in our lives. God leads us through many unfamiliar places, and our Rule of Life should embrace the rhythm of God's leading. Every part of our journey, even the valley of the shadow of death, will change and deepen us if we go through it with Jesus.

Embracing rhythm means that we avoid ruts and we refuse to make icons into idols. When we become too attached to nonessentials, God will lead us to new places where we learn again to trust in him instead of other things.

When you develop a spiritual growth plan or Rule of Life, include flexibility for the changing seasons of your spiritual life. Update your Rule as needed rather than rigidly adhering to a plan that was right for a different period of your life. Be open to changes in your usual spiritual or worship routines. Include not only demanding goals but restful and restorative ones.

In my own Rule of Life I set a goal of taking a personal half-day retreat at least six times a year. I haven't always managed to do it, but I don't beat up on myself when I fail. I still like to keep the goal before me as a reminder to set aside time for renewal.

As I write this, the church year is entering another season of Lent, and I am considering what disciplines or exercises will help me grow during this penitent time. Such seasons offer a wonderful opportunity to attend to neglected areas of spiritual development. I know that Lent will last only six weeks, which makes the changes seem more manageable.

During Lent I set short-term goals and disciplines which are meant only for that brief season of my spiritual life. Many people follow Jesus' example of engaging in periods of fasting and frequent prayer during Lent or at other times when the Holy Spirit calls them to increased spiritual focus. A spiritual life that does not leave room for rhythm and flexibility runs the danger of stagnation.

A Rule should work with, not against, a person's individual temperament. There is no one-size-fits-all spiritual Rule of Life. The Rule of Benedict is the best known of the systems for Christian religious orders that developed over the last two millennia. Other orders developed their own rules. The Augustinians, Carmelites, Dominicans, Franciscans and Jesuits are only a few of the other orders who defined themselves by different sets of priorities.

If a person has a Franciscan temperament, a highly structured schedule of prayer and Bible study might be stifling, where a person of Thomistic temperament might thrive on such a Rule. At the same time the person with the Franciscan temperament, who craves more sensual forms of worship, might do well to stretch herself or himself through a disciplined rubric of prayer and study.

My own Rule of Life includes this goal: "I will spend an hour in Scripture reading, devotional reading and prayer at least four mornings per week." I love time alone in contemplative prayer, but in my busyness it is often the first thing to go. I need a reminder to keep it as part of my life.

A spiritual Rule should address one's signature sins. The purpose of naming our signature sins and their antidotes is to provide a map toward greater wholeness and holiness.

Write down your signature sins and their antidotes. Then set the list aside. As the Holy Spirit leads, add new sins and antidotes to the list. One of the most useful disciplines for a Rule of Life is commitment to regular confession of one's signature sins and regular supplication for their antidotes. In my Rule of Life one goal particularly focuses on this need: "I will regularly confess my signature sins and ask God to reorient my loves."

As I said earlier, the regular confession of my signature sins brought on a powerful season of transformation for me. Although it was painful, I found it freeing rather than burdensome. I experienced a period of about a year where God led me through an intensive season of self-examination. No period since then has brought the same intensity of awareness. Trust the rhythm of your spiritual life. The darkest nights are usually followed by the brightest periods of illumination.

In earlier chapters we discussed the fallen human tendency to place inordinate importance on either the spirit or the body. It is difficult to maintain a balanced respect for the needs of both. In developing a spiritual Rule of Life, it is tempting to put all the emphasis on internal spiritual needs and neglect the fact that we are embodied creatures. We should respect and care for the physical body as the temple of the Holy Spirit.

A healthy Rule should care for the needs of the body. Rest, exercise, hygiene, healthy eating and abandonment of unhealthy habits should have an important part in a Rule of Life. It is hypocritical to make goals of increased time in prayer while doing nothing about addiction to alcohol or cigarettes. It is fine to attend to spiritual sloth as long as one is also addressing excess time on the couch in front of the TV. In my own Rule I have a goal for this area: "I will begin and seek to improve a manageable pattern of exercise."

Western Christian spirituality has become inordinately focused on each individual. Many Christians shop for the church that is most entertaining or best equipped to meet their needs, but they do not consider their responsibility to the life of the congregation. Unfortunately the modern buffet of churches and worship styles only serves to promote the idea of the believer as an isolated consumer.

Investment in a worshiping community goes beyond Sunday. It goes beyond those events that happen in the church building. It even goes beyond small groups, as helpful as they are. An incarnational Christian life focuses on how we represent Christ to the world at all times. Such living requires being fed and supported by more than individual devotions and Sunday sermons. Fellowship with other believers is essential to maintaining spiritual health. We need communal life with the body of Christ in order to grow toward maturity in Christ.

The first and most important church is in our own home. Our wives, husbands, children, parents and siblings are first and foremost our sisters and brothers in Christ. Our Rule of Life should include the commitment to pray, study and worship as a family. Caring for oneself or even for the rest of the world means nothing if we neglect our own loved ones. Jesus had a special place in his heart for widows and orphans, people cut off from a family to care for them. In our time I believe he challenges the church to make sure that no one in our church family is left alone and drifting between Sunday services.

Worshiping and praying with other believers is a powerful source of spiritual nourishment. Unfortunately, the church is also the source of our deepest spiritual wounds. Even the healthiest congregation eventually goes through some crisis that drives some members away and leaves others feeling hurt. Despite the painful reality of church hurts, a Rule of Life should foster commitment to a community of believers, not only to individual spiritual development. The community may be small. Communion may take place with only two, because Jesus is in their midst. A prayer group or Sunday school class can become both family and community.

In your Rule of Life, make a commitment to worship, pray and be formed within community. If you have no community, make a commitment to allow God to lead you to one or to create one. No one is an island, and souls that grow in isolation lack the supporting structure of a community to sustain them through spiritually difficult times. If you have no church community, consider adding a Rule to seek one. You might also consider including a Rule such as "I will prayerfully seek a spiritual director."

HEARTS SET ON PILGRIMAGE

I hope the reader is left with excitement for the way of the pilgrim rather than a sense of guilt or heaviness about the spiritual journey. As the psalmist said, "Blessed are those whose strength is in you, / who have set their hearts on pilgrimage" (Ps 84:5). I have been blessed to know many wonderful people, including students, patients and friends, that have walked with me, and I with them, on pilgrimage.

A pilgrimage blesses in unexpected ways. The blessing of the journey usually looks nothing like we thought it would look. It usually arrives in a changed heart. Often the least wanted or most surprising parts of the journey leave the greatest gifts. The journey of seeking to know, confront and transform our signature sins stretches our faith in God's goodness.

We have God's promise that "if we confess our sins, he is faithful and just and will forgive us our sins and purify us from all unrighteousness" (1 Jn 1:9). A pilgrimage which begins with the confession of sin will lead to righteousness. If our hearts are set on pilgrimage, God promises to make sure the route brings us to him.

Unlike literal pilgrimages to a holy site, the most striking thing about the pilgrimage of the spiritual life is that one can know it and describe it only from some point along the way. I have experienced and described many spiritual adventures and accompanied many people on portions of their spiritual pilgrimage. Yet my own pilgrimage is not done, and neither is yours. Like Abraham and the other pilgrims memorialized in Hebrews 11, I have seen the holy city only from a distance, on the horizon.

You and I can share our stories of the journey and of our glimpses of the distant city. The focus of our spiritual journey is found in the fact that our Lord Jesus Christ has gone on to prepare a place for us and that he will one day return to usher us into that place (Jn 14:1-3). That is why Paul asserts, "If only for this life we have hope in Christ, we are to be pitied more than all men" (1 Cor 15:19). If the city on the horizon is a mirage, our faith is in vain. If Christ was not raised from the dead, we are only cowards who cling to a comforting myth and encourage each other in a shared delusion.

This metaphor of a shared delusion speaks powerfully to me as a clinical psychologist. I deal in delusions every day. I make a living by dismantling delusions. In most people's minds truth and illusion have become so intertwined that I feel like a surgeon trying to remove a tumor without damaging the surrounding nerves. My task is made more complex by the reality that I cannot actually do the surgery. I must help my patients to do it themselves.

Delusions are seductive. They promise comfort and relief from pain. Like all lies they eventually enslave us, as we must deny more and more of the truth to maintain them. The truth always sets us free, even if we must go through pain to find it.

We are always becoming who we are. Though we may spend our lives hiding the loves that reside in the depths of our hearts, eventually they will be fully exposed. We should be very careful what we allow to take root there. Sins, like weeds, insinuate themselves into every corner of our souls. The pilgrimage toward Christ requires bushwhacking, cutting away the sinful hindrances to our progress.

THE SOUL'S GREATEST LOVE

If I accept Christ's invitation to allow my heart to be born again in him, to die with him and to be raised to new life with him, my destination is secure. The end of my pilgrimage is determined from the beginning. I've been hooked and Christ is continually reeling me in, even when I struggle and pull away. Our pilgrimage will always end in the soul's greatest love, that by which it has been hooked. We become formed into the likeness of that to which we have attached our love. If what we love is a delusion constructed to provide us with comfort, we will become hollow people, empty like the delusions we have worshiped, to be pitied more than all others.

If what we love is the Lord Jesus Christ, we will become Christlike people. Our signature sins will be redeemed into strengths and talents worthy of being presented as gifts to our master when we arrive at his city.

My pilgrimage has drawn me ever more toward Jesus Christ. I look back and see at every turn along the way what I could not see at the time: the path always leads toward Christ. Through the disciplines and practices that I have shared in this book, disciplines and practices passed down from centuries of fellow pilgrims, the call of Christ has become deeper and ever more compelling. Unlike delusions, the call of Christ grows stronger when it is questioned or challenged, more tangible when it is examined. It sustains me in times of drought and is no less sweet in times of abundance. It does not require me to defend it, because it defends me.

I hope you have become excited to begin or continue your pilgrimage of seeking after righteousness. If you strive to know and confess your signature sins and to humbly ask God to provide the antidotes, you will surely and steadily be reeled in toward Christ. Even your greatest struggles to pull away only delay the inevitable. We become transformed into the likeness of that which we love, and there is no one more worthy of our love than Jesus.

TAMING YOUR WAYWARD HEART

- Have you ever had a plan for your spiritual formation? Is that idea foreign to you?

- Which is more important to you, depth or happiness?

- Have you ever resented the fact that God would give you no guarantee of health or happiness?

    Have you ever been tempted by the health and wealth gospel which promises success and happiness to Christians who have enough faith?

- Try the spiritual exercise of meditating on yourself as an old man or old woman. Quiet yourself and picture the kind of scene where you might be someday after retirement. Now imagine yourself as an old man or old woman. Stand off at a distance, watching yourself. Where are you? Who are you with? How do you act? Walk up to your old self and sit down to have a talk. What would your old self say to you? What would you say to your old self?

- If you were to die today, what would be said about you? Write an honest and accurate eulogy.

- In your journal describe the person you wish you would someday be. Write the eulogy you wish would someday be true of you.

- What is different between the person you hope you will someday be and the person you are today?

  What needs to happen between now and then to bring that person into being?

  What are the steps to reaching those goals?

- In your journal write the first draft of your Rule of Life, keeping in mind that it will evolve over time.

  In what ways should your Rule seek balance?

  In what ways should your Rule embrace rhythm?

  How should your Rule work with your temperament?

  How should your Rule help you confess and remain mindful of your signature sins? What antidotes to sin should you pray for?

  How will your Rule include caring for your body?

  What needs for community should your Rule address?

Questions for Group Discussion

THIS BOOK GREW IN PART FROM MY OWN experience in an ongoing spiritual formation group. I believe in the power of such groups to transform their members. I hope this book will help some groups get started and other groups go deeper in their support of each other's spiritual lives.

Because every group is different, there is no one-size-fits-all way to use a book like this in a group context. Your group should adapt the following questions for your own use. After you have read a chapter, you could use the questions as a jumping-off point for discussion. If the group has a limited time to meet and is prone to lively discussions, it will be wise to ask for everyone's opinion of which one or two questions are most helpful or intriguing, then begin with them and get to the others as time allows.

Some questions require more vulnerability than others. No one should be pressured to answer any question which is too uncomfortable. Your group should try to find a happy medium where no one is completely unwilling to share and no one feels inappropriately vulnerable. A group member should not make others feel awkward by voicing details that are too intimate or by demanding more than their share of the group's attention. Everyone in the group should promise privacy and confidentiality so no one needs to fear personal stories being told outside the group. Most important, no one should judge or condemn another group member. Maintain an atmosphere of grace, safety and trust at all times.

CHAPTER 1: WHY DO WE SIN?

1. Before reading this chapter, how would you have answered the question of why we sin?

2. How has your thinking changed about why we sin?

3. With whom do you most identify in Jesus' story of the lost son: the prodigal, the older brother or the father? Why?

4. What are some examples of ways we should respond differently to some people's sins than to others'?

5. When have you realized that what you know about God is out of sync with how you feel toward God?

   Talk about times when you have questions about God.

6. Do you believe it is possible to attain a state of sinlessness in this life? Why or why not?

7. What do you feel makes a church or other Christian community a safe place to confess your sins?

8. Have you experienced a time when God did not answer your prayer or when God's answer disappointed you?

   How did your experience affect your relationship with God?

9. Dallas Willard confronts the church's tendency to create "gospels of sin management" when we focus on behavior rather than the

state of the heart. How have you seen this tendency in the church and/or in your own life?

10. What issues of faith do you see being treated with greater or lesser importance than they deserve?

11. Which type of heresy would you find more tempting: the denial of Jesus' humanity or the denial of Jesus' deity? Why?

12. Do you agree that men and women struggle differently with pride and fear?

Chapter 2: Pride, Envy, Anger and Gluttony

1. Pride is often described as the foundational sin. How does pride show up differently for women than for men?

2. Which form of pride causes more destruction: inward pride or outward pride?

   Why do you think that is true?

3. What form of envy do you see most in our culture or in your social world?

4. How does the advertising industry promote envy?

5. How is anger different from the other sins?

6. What does righteous anger look like?

   How is it different from the anger most people usually feel?

7. Can inability or refusal to be angry ever be a sin? Why or why not?

8. Have you ever fasted for spiritual purposes?

If you have, how did it affect you spiritually?

9. What pleasure is most in danger of becoming gluttonous for you?

CHAPTER 3: LUST, GREED, SLOTH AND FEAR

1. Which do you think causes more harm in the world, lust or anger? Why?

2. How does the sin of prudery cause harm?

3. How have you seen differences over money cause conflict in marital relationships?

4. Do you think it is acceptable for Christians to seek to be wealthy? How would you qualify your answer?

5. How is this chapter's description of sloth different from how you have understood this sin?

6. Do you agree that sadness can be a sinful form of sloth? Why or why not?

7. Do you agree that fear can be sinful? Why or why not?

8. Are there any fears that continue to plague you after your experience of God's faithfulness should have dispelled them?

CHAPTER 4: NAMING OUR SIGNATURE SINS

1. When have you had an experience like Eustace's experience when Aslan cut away the layers of dragon scales, when God stripped away layers of your old self and brought about a significant transformation into a new person?

2. Do you feel that you sin in unpredictable ways or in consistent patterns?

   If your sin has consistent patterns, what are they?

3. In your experience of the institutional church (congregations of which you have been a part) how safe was it for someone to openly confess sin and ask for support in combating sin?

4. To what extent do you agree that mourning is necessary for spiritual growth?

   To what extent does the church promote this teaching?

5. Are you willing to commit to a period of consistent daily prayer that God will help you name and acknowledge your primary signature sin(s)?

   Are you willing to share your experience with someone else and allow that person to hold you accountable?

CHAPTER 5: TEMPERAMENT AND SIN

1. What are some evidences that God delights in diversity?

2. Talk about a kind of diversity in the body of Christ (the church) that you or others have difficulty delighting in.

3. Discuss any ways that you feel that others in the church do not appreciate your uniqueness.

4. Do you believe that some people's temperament makes it more difficult for them to resist sin? Why or why not?

5. Which of the four spiritual temperament categories—Ignatian, Franciscan, Augustinian and Thomistic—fits you best?

Do other people agree with your evaluation?

6. Without revealing your opinion, ask someone who knows you well which spiritual temperament best describes you.

7. Which one or two of the Enneagram types sounds most like you? Why?

8. How does your temperament affect your patterns of temptation and sin?

9. How does God parent you differently than someone else with a different temperament?

Chapter 6: Culture, Ethnicity and Sin

1. What is your culture? Who are your people? Make your answer as specific as possible. Consider region (South, East Coast, Appalachia, etc.), religious subculture (evangelical, Catholic, etc.), ethnic roots (Norwegian descent, third-generation Polish, etc.), socio-economic background (blue collar, "old money," etc.) and population density (rural, suburban or urban).

2. How has your culture influenced the ways you are tempted or not tempted to sin?

3. Ask someone from another culture to help you receive a glimpse of your culture through his or her eyes. Be careful to hear the observer's description without becoming defensive.

4. Where you live and work, are you ethnically in the majority or in the minority?

What does it feel like when you find yourself in the opposite context?

5. With what race or ethnicity do you primarily identify?

   What are some of the primary sins of that group?

6. Do you identify with the primary ways your culture defines gender roles and expectations, or do chafe under those expectations?

CHAPTER 7: GENDER, FAMILY AND SIN

1. How has your gender influenced the ways that you sin?

2. In a mixed gender group, discuss the perceptions each gender has of the other.

3. What advantages does each gender have in society?

   What disadvantages does each gender have?

4. Do you agree with the author's premise that the discussion of the sin of anger must be different for women than for men? Why or why not?

5. What do you most value about being the gender that you are?

   What do you most value from the opposite gender?

6. What are the patterns of sin that run through your family?

7. How have you broken free from some of the "curses" of your family?

   What family sins do you still want to break free from?

8. What are the gifts and strengths of your family legacy?

CHAPTER 8: THE BIOLOGY OF SIN

1. How should the realization that our bodies are integral to who we are as souls affect the ways that we treat our bodies?

2. Do you experience biologically based limitations or struggles that affect your spiritual life? If yes, how so? If no, how does that affect your empathy for those who have such struggles?

3. In what ways do you see the addiction to comfort in our culture or in the church?

4. What is your attitude toward Christians using antidepressant medication?

   Do you agree that antidepressant medication should be embraced as an important way that science has helped to redeem the effects of the Fall? Why or why not?

5. How has pain in your life led to greater spiritual growth?

6. Have you ever prayed for or witnessed miraculous healing? If so, how has it affected your spiritual life?

7. How should biological factors influence the extent to which we hold others or ourselves accountable for sin?

CHAPTER 9: SPIRITUAL DISCIPLINES TO TAME THE WAYWARD HEART

1. How have you seen the denial of death at work in your own family/church/community?

2. Do you know anyone (including yourself) who has expressed thankfulness for a trial, persecution, disease or another form of suffering?

   How has it affected your faith?

3. Do you practice any forms of ascetic spiritual disciplines? If yes, how has it affected your spiritual life? If no, what practice could

you commit to in the near future?

4. What is the experience of silence and solitude like for you?

   Is it welcome or difficult?

5. How do you feel about the idea that a loving God would withdraw from us or allow us to experience pain to stimulate our growth?

6. Try meditating on longing. As a group, listen with eyes closed to a song about longing for heaven. Imagine what heaven will be like.

7. What do you think of the idea that we are called to be discontented, always remembering that we are aliens who are just passing through?

   If you embraced this idea, how would it change your life?

8. What happens when we focus on salvation to the exclusion of sanctification?

   Was your spiritual upbringing slanted in either direction?

9. What is the positive side of your signature sin?

   How do you see it being redeemed into a gift?

10. If it is true that "pain is the most reliable map to the place where God is at work in a person's life," where is God at work in your life?

11. Spend time praying and seeking the name of the antidote for your central signature sin. The name is often difficult to swallow.

    How would your life be different if the antidote became your central virtue?

12. In addition to praying for God to give you the antidote for your sin, what spiritual disciplines might help that virtue grow in your life?

Chapter 10: Formation in Community

1. What is your community history?

   What communities have you belonged to and how healthy were they?

2. What does community mean to you?

   What positive and negative images come to mind?

3. Can you think of an example of a time when your experience of community smoothed some rough place in you?

4. Is there some connection to rural life in your family history?

   How far back?

   How do those roots (or lack thereof) affect you now?

5. "For most people in our culture anonymity is the default condition; community is an option." How have you found this statement to be true or untrue?

6. Are you in a healthy spiritual community now?

   If you are, thank God for those people. If you are not, how can you take steps to find or create a spiritual community?

Chapter 11: Spiritual Rhythms of Sin and Grace

1. Is the path of your spiritual development more like a straight line or a curving helix?

Why do you answer as you do?

2. What have been the key periods of purgation in your life?

   How did they change you spiritually?

3. During the stage of illumination, spiritual things seem clearer. Describe a time of illumination when you were on a spiritual mountaintop.

4. When have you witnessed anyone claiming a new illumination from God that seemed to violate scriptural principles?

   How did you discern the error?

5. During a unitive period we feel a sense of living in harmony with God. Do you feel that kind of shalom now? If not, how long has it been since you felt that way?

6. How do you respond to the idea that God sometimes moves away from us?

   If you have experienced such times, how have they affected your faith?

CHAPTER 12: RESTORING SPIRITUAL BALANCE

1. What are the positive and negative aspects of denominationalism and other different streams within the Christian church?

2. Were you taught to fear or distrust any of the spiritual streams?

   How were those streams presented to you?

3. Which of the spiritual streams is your strongest spoke and/or the one that most comforts you?

4. Which of the spiritual streams are your weakest spokes, the ones that stretch you most? Why?

5. How is God calling you to embrace balance and/or rhythm in your spiritual life?

Chapter 13: Becoming Who We Are in Christ

1. If you were to recount your spiritual pilgrimage, what have been the most significant defining moments along the way?

   Are you currently on the road or are you resting at an oasis?

2. Where do you see the most active struggle between depth and superficiality within the church?

3. Take a few minutes and meditate on yourself as an old man or old woman as described in the chapter. What does your old self have to say to you?

4. If you imagine the kind of old woman or old man you want to be, how does your current life need to change in order to lead in that direction?

5. Was the idea of a Rule of Life initially attractive or oppressive to you? Why?

6. After you have created a Rule of Life, share all or some of it with a spiritual friend or group. How does their reaction confirm or challenge your Rule?

7. What is the single most challenging or helpful thing you have taken from this book that will influence the next stage of your spiritual pilgrimage?

Acknowledgments

Many people deserve thanks and acknowledgment for their parts in the creation of this work. For more than a decade, my wife, Patti Hughes Mangis, and I have taught workshops and led spiritual formation retreats together, and this book grew out of that collaboration. So Patti's DNA is throughout this book. Our friend Bob Watson also taught with us, and shaped our thinking about these ideas.

Over the last few years, my son Josh has patiently endured many hours when my attention was focused on writing and not on him. He has graciously allowed me to share stories about him.

I also want to thank many of my graduate students who over the years read early drafts, discussed the ideas that I presented and even recommended thoughtful discussion questions to include in the book. Nicole Saylor was instrumental in the latter regard.

A significant theme of this book is the importance of community for spiritual formation. Much of my understanding of how a community can contribute to such formation comes from my own experience in a fellowship that has met together for fourteen years. I am grateful for these people who have truly become my family in Christ: Marian Oliver, Lee and Linda Joiner, David and L. B. Norton, John and Jane Stoller-Schoff, and Brad and Kathy Cathey.

During the final proofreading stage of this book, four months before it was due out in the bookstores, I suffered a debilitating stroke. With the patience and support of my editor, Cynthia Bunch, these people brought the book to completion: my wife, Patti; our dear friends Cynthia Neal Kimball, Rich Butman and L. B. Norton; and graduate student Amanda Blackburn.

Notes

Chapter 1: Why Do We Sin?

p. 11   In his wonderful book: Henri J. M. Nouwen, *The Return of the Prodigal Son* (New York: Doubleday, 1992).

p. 15   "gospels of sin management": Dallas Willard, *The Divine Conspiracy: Rediscovering Our Hidden Life in God* (San Francisco: HarperSanFrancisco, 1998).

p. 16   "Most merciful God": Church of England, The 1979 Book of Common Prayer (London: Oxford University Press, 1979), p. 360, emphasis added.

p. 17   in fact I have patients: I prefer the term *patient*, which historically meant "one who patiently endures their affliction," to the more frequently used term *client*, which connotes a business transaction.

p. 19   "an incurable suspicion of God": Oswald Chambers, *The Philosophy of Sin: How to Deal with Moral Problems* (London: Marshall, Morgan, & Scott, 1960), p. 13.

p. 20   the psychoanalyst Ana-Maria Rizzuto wrote: Ana-Maria Rizzuto, *The Birth of the Living God: A Psychoanalytic Study* (Chicago: University of Chicago Press, 1979).

p. 22   "self-knowledge": John of the Cross, *The Dark Night of the Soul* (New York: Doubleday, 1990), p. 80.

p. 24   Stewart notes that: Columba Stewart, "The Desert Fathers on Radical Self-Honesty," *Vox Benedictina* 8 (1991).

p. 25   "Oh begin!": John Wesley, *The Works of the Rev. John Wesley: Volume 4* (Chestnut Hill, Mass.: Adamant Media Corporation, 2006), p. 49.

Chapter 2: Pride, Envy, Anger and Gluttony

p. 27   I have especially been helped: Loren Gavitt, ed., *Saint Augustine's Prayer Book: A Book of Devotion for Members of the Episcopal Church* (New York: Holy Cross Publications, 1976).

p. 28   C. S. Lewis wrote an allegory: C. S. Lewis, *The Great Divorce* (New York: MacMillan, 1996), pp. 104-5.

p. 30   Thomas Aquinas noted: St. Thomas Aquinas *Summa Theologiae* 1-2.77.4a.

p. 35   "The deadly poison": Philip Schaff, *Sulpitius Severus, Vincent of Lerins and John Cassian*, A Select Library of Nicene and Post-Nicene Fathers of the Christian Church, Second Series, vol. 11 (Grand Rapids: Christian Classics Ethereal Library, 1973).

Chapter 3: Lust, Greed, Sloth and Fear

p. 48   corporate raider Gordon Gekko: *Wall Street*, dir. Oliver Stone (USA: 20th Century Fox, 1987).

Chapter 4: Naming Our Signature Sins

p. 66   Eustace Scrubb undergoes: C. S. Lewis, *The Voyage of the "Dawn Treader"* (New York: Collier, 1952), p. 88.

Chapter 5: Temperament and Sin

p. 80   Jung understood temperaments: Many Christians distrust Jung based on his explorations into the mystical realms of spirituality. His character typologies are observations about categories of human temperament and behavior. They should not be dismissed out of hand because of other things Jung wrote and believed.

p. 81   One helpful review: Chester P. Michael and Marie C. Norrisey,

Prayer and Temperament: Different Prayer Forms for Different Personality Types (Charlottesville, Va.: Open Door, 1991). The authors use the Jungian/Myers-Briggs typologies to identify four common categories of temperament, named in honor of four spiritual giants who exhibited them, and to outline spiritual practices that are helpful for each type. Other useful resources using the same typologies: Chester P. Michael, *An Introduction to Spiritual Direction: A Psychological Approach for Directors and Directees* (New York: Paulist Press, 2004); M. Robert Mulholland Jr., *Invitation to a Journey: A Road Map for Spiritual Formation* (Downers Grove, Ill.: InterVarsity Press, 1993); Marchiene Vroon Rienstra, *Come to the Feast: Seeking God's Bounty for Our Lives and Souls* (Grand Rapids: Eerdmans, 1995).

p. 92   I have used several common titles: Two key resources for exploring the Enneagram are Richard Rohr and Andreas Ebert, *The Enneagram: A Christian Perspective,* trans. Peter Heinegg (New York: Crossroad, 2001), and Suzanne Zuercher, *Enneagram Spirituality: From Compulsion to Contemplation* (Notre Dame, Ind.: Ave Maria Press, 1992).

p. 96   "Someone may fear": A. W. Tozer, *The Pursuit of God* (Camp Hill, Penn.: Christian Publications, 1982), p. 87.

Chapter 7: Gender, Family and Sin

p. 111   One of the most articulate discussions: Mary Stewart Van Leeuwen, "Christian Maturity in Light of Feminist Theory," *Journal of Psychology and Theology* 16, no. 2 (1988); Mary Stewart Van Leeuwen, *Gender & Grace: Love, Work & Parenting in a Changing World* (Downers Grove, Ill.: InterVarsity Press, 1990).

p. 115   Several years ago: Cynthia J. Neal and Michael W. Mangis, "Unwanted Sexual Experiences Among Christian College Women: Saying No on the Inside," *Journal of Psychology and Theology* 23, no. 3 (1995).

p. 116   As noted earlier: Van Leeuwen, "Christian Maturity in Light of Feminist Theory."

p. 121   In her song "Generations": Sara Groves, *Conversations* (Mobile, Ala.: Integrity Media, 2001).

Chapter 9: Spiritual Disciplines to Tame the Wayward Heart

p. 144   "all the unhappiness": Blaise Pascal, "Thoughts," Collier & Son <www.bartleby.com/48/1>.

p. 147   Dallas Willard in his compelling book: Dallas Willard, *The Divine Conspiracy: Rediscovering Our Hidden Life in God* (San Francisco: HarperSanFrancisco, 1998).

p. 151   I recently read: Dennis McDougal, "The Mavens Speak: When Celebrities Insert Both Feet," August 9, 2006 <www.nytimes.com>.

p. 161   A daily time of devotion: For an excellent guide to daily prayer and Scripture reading I recommend Rueben P. Job and Norman Shawchuck, *A Guide to Prayer for Ministers and Other Servants* (Nashville: Upper Room, 1983).

p. 162   directing our "naked intent": *The Cloud of Unknowing*, trans. Clifton Wolters (New York: Penguin, 1978).

Chapter 10: Formation in Community

p. 165   Years ago I read: Dietrich Bonhoeffer, *Life Together* (New York: Harper, 1954).

p. 170   Renovaré provides a practical: James Bryan Smith and Lynda L. Graybeal, *A Spiritual Formation Workbook: Small-Group Resources for Nurturing Christian Growth* (San Francisco: HarperSanFrancisco, 1993).

p. 171   The other type of group: Rose Mary Dougherty, *Group Spiritual Direction: Community for Discernment* (New York: Paulist Press, 1995).

Chapter 11: Spiritual Rhythms of Sin and Grace

p. 181   the sixteenth-century monk: John of the Cross, *The Dark Night of the Soul* <www.ccel.org/ccel/john_cross/dark_night.html>.

Chapter 12: Restoring Spiritual Balance

p. 197   six streams of spirituality: Richard J. Foster, *Streams of Living Water: Celebrating the Great Traditions of Christian Faith* (San Francisco: HarperSanFrancisco, 1998).

p. 200   In an exercise: James Bryan Smith and Lynda L. Graybeal, *A Spiritual Formation Workbook: Small-Group Resources for Nurturing Christian Growth* (San Francisco: HarperSanFrancisco, 1993).

Chapter 13: Becoming Who We Are in Christ

p. 216   "Turn your eyes": Helen Howarth Lemmel, "O Soul, Are You Weary and Troubled?" c. 1922. Renewal 1950 by H. H. Lemmel. Assigned to Singspiration, Inc./ASCAP. Benson Company, Inc., Nashville.

p. 217   There are helpful resources: Ruth Haley Barton, *Sacred Rhythms: Arranging Our Lives for Spiritual Transformation* (Downers Grove, Ill.: InterVarsity Press, 2006); Marjorie J. Thompson, *Soul Feast: An Invitation to the Christian Spiritual Life* (Louisville, Ky.: Westminster John Knox Press, 1995).

formatio

TRADITION. EXPERIENCE.
TRANSFORMATION.

Formatio books from InterVarsity Press follow the rich tradition of the church in the journey of spiritual formation. These books are not merely about being informed, but about being transformed by Christ and conformed to his image. Formatio stands in InterVarsity Press's evangelical publishing tradition by integrating God's Word with spiritual practice and by prompting readers to move from inward change to outward witness. InterVarsity Press uses the chambered nautilus for Formatio, a symbol of spiritual formation because of its continual spiral journey outward as it moves from its center. We believe that each of us is made with a deep desire to be in God's presence. Formatio books help us to fulfill our deepest desires and to become our true selves in light of God's grace.